Contents

Preface

Dr. Siebert Q. Duntley, who was a professor at the Massachusetts Institute of Technology, founded the Visibility Laboratory (Vis Lab) at MIT. In 1952 he moved the Vis Lab to San Diego where it became a research lab of the Scripps Institution of Oceanography, University of California. Dr. Duntley served as the Laboratory Director until his retirement in 1977. It was my good fortune to join the staff of the Vis Lab in 1954. I spent 25 years with the lab, becoming the Laboratory Director at the time of Dr. Duntley's retirement. The Vis Lab designed and constructed equipment to allow documentation of the transmission of light in the atmosphere and in the water. It also had a vision research facility where experiments were performed to document the capabilities and limitations of the human visual system. The Vis Lab had a great staff that displayed a sincere belief that successful research was a team effort, thus generating a friendly atmosphere that made each of us look forward to coming to work each morning. One of the goals of the laboratory was to develop what we thought of as "Visibility Engineering," the application of the results of the research to real world problems.

During the early space flight program, questions arose as to whether prolonged weightlessness would result in reduction in the visual performance capability of the astronauts involved in the flights. The Vis Lab was the lead laboratory in what was referred to as the "Visual Acuity" experiments to be conducted on Gemini V and Gemini VII flights in 1965. The Vis Lab built equipment that was carried on board to allow the astronauts to measure their visual acuity throughout the flights. The lab also set up ground targets in Texas and Australia to allow "out the window" testing as well. This association with NASA led to the Vis Lab receiving a series of grants from NASA to study the role of vision in accidents involving the collision of two aircraft. I was named the Principal Investigator on those grants. I also served as the Principal Investigator on a contract with the FAA to extend these studies to include the visual aspects of the "Avoid" portion of "See and Avoid."

As a result of these aircraft collision studies, I received a call from the Department of Justice in Washington, D.C., in 1971, requesting that I serve as an expert in litigation associated with a midair collision in California. That led to my being called upon to perform similar services in other aircraft accidents. To date, I have served as an expert in 120 midair collision cases. These expert witness experiences led to my being called upon to serve as an expert in a variety of other types of accidents where visibility issues were involved. This included aircraft wire strikes, railroad crossing accidents, and a variety of automobile and pedestrian accidents. In 1979, I took an early retirement from the University of California and established Harris Visibility Studies, Inc., to pursue these accident studies on a full-time basis.

My son, James L. Harris II, is a coauthor of this book. Jim II began working with me on a part-time basis while he was still in high school in 1979. Upon graduation from high school in 1982, he became a full time employee of HVSI. From 1985 to 1991 he served in the United States Air Force and as an employee at the North Island Naval Air Station Depot. In 1991 I convinced him to return to HVSI as a full time employee. We had a terrific father-son relationship. I looked forward with a smile to his arrival at work each morning. He very quickly demonstrated his skills with the computer, including the generation of animations of accident scenarios. He also showed great capability in handling photographic assignments, including the computer correction of the resulting imagery in order to achieve accurate representation of accident scenes. He did an excellent job of learning the technical aspects of visibility issues associated with accidents. He was also an excellent aid in pointing out the specifics of technical visibility issues that I took for granted because of my long involvement in such matters, but that actually required detailed explanation to achieve general understanding by those not familiar with the technical details. He was not only a great coworker and my son, but a great friend as well. We frequently discussed our desire to publish a book on forensic visibility. We spent a substantial period of time in discussing and outlining the details of the contents of such a book. We were very pleased when Lawyers & Judges Publishing agreed to publish this book, which we would co-author.

Unfortunately, Jim II died in September 2009. Dealing with this unexpected event has been extremely difficult for me. As of January 2010, I elected to take on no new accident cases. I made this decision because I wanted my primary priority to be associated with the completion of this book. I felt that accomplishing this objective was the best action that I could take to honor the memory of Jim II.

I would also like to express my great appreciation to my son, Mike, who, upon Jim II's death, volunteered to assist in editing the book. He has been a great aid in dealing with my sometimes-twisted grammar and my failure to offer adequate explanation of technical matters. His assistance has been of great value to me. Finally, I am grateful to Eric Salo of Lawyers & Judges Publishing for his patience, timely suggestions, and excellent editing, paving the road to achieving the goal of publishing this book.

I would like to offer a couple of comments with respect to the contents of this book. I have made an effort to limit the material to those topics where my background and experience provide a legitimate basis for passing along information that may be of assistance. This is not a textbook where every aspect of each subject needs to be addressed. Nor is there any need for me to discuss topics that have been well covered by other authors. I am a mathematically oriented engineer. I recognize that equations and graphs may not be at all helpful to some readers. For them, I have attempted, as best I can, to offer a verbal interpretation. I hope that those readers can simply pass over the mathematical approach. For the mathematically inclined, I hope you can take in the equations and graphs and not be offended by the redundancy associated with my verbal explanations.

Throughout this writing I have used U.S. units of measurement. The following tables is for those who prefer metric system units:

U.S. and Metric Conversion Chart

Distance

1 inch	2.54 centimeters	
1 foot	0.3048 meters	
1 statute mile	5280 feet	1609.3 meters
1 nautical mile	6076 feet	1852.0 meters

Velocity

1 mile per hour	1.6093 kilometers/hour
1 knot	1.852 kilometers/hour

Angle

1 degree	2pi/360 radians	
1 arc minute	1/60 deg	2pi/21600 radians

Optical

1 candela	1 lumen/steradian	
1 foot candle	1 lumen/sq ft	10.76 lux
1 foot Lambert	1/pi candela/sq ft	1.1×10^{-3} lamberts

—James L. Harris, Sr.

Chapter 1

The Human Visual System

1.1 Introduction

As children we are taught many subjects but, generally speaking, how to use our eyes and the limitations associated with our visual system is not one of those topics. The fact is that most of us learn to use our eyes by personal experience and we end up doing a pretty good job of it. However, we tend to become adults without having a clear understanding of the capabilities and limitations of our visual system. This can influence our attempts to realistically evaluate accidents associated with an individual's ability to successfully perform some visual task. The human visual system is very complex. In this section, no attempt will be made to explore the detailed anatomical structure of the human eye. This section will deal only with those properties of the normal eye that are important to developing some understanding of visual performance.

1.2 The Lens System

The human eye has a two-part lens system that images the scene on an array of

1

photosensitive receptors, somewhat like a digital camera. The outermost component of the lens system is the cornea. The cornea has no focusing capability. The lens is located somewhat behind the cornea. In a camera, focus is accomplished by changing the position of the lens. In the eye, focus is accomplished by muscles that alter the shape and thickness of the lens. This provides the capability to alter the power of the lens in order to focus on an object at a selected distance. One limitation of this focus system is that the lens tends to stiffen with age, limiting the range of distances over which focus can be accomplished. As we grow older this leads to the need for prescription glasses to supplement the focus for either near or far targets. Ultimately in the aging process, the lens stiffens to the degree that the focus is fixed at one distance and glasses are required for all other viewing distances. When you observe an individual who takes off glasses to view an object at close distance, this individual is *near sighted*, whereas if an individual puts on glasses to view an object at close distance, this individual is *far sighted*. Some individuals have a lens system with focus fixed at a distance beyond infinity, and they require prescription glasses for viewing at all distances. It is sometimes helpful in accident analysis to generate an image that illustrates the extent of the image blur associated with improper focus for an individual with a specified visual acuity score, in order to aid in determining whether this could have been the cause of a failure to see some important detail related to an accident. It should also be noted that when vision takes place at lower light levels, the pupil diameter increases as a means of supplying more light to the image. The amount of the image blur increases with pupil diameter, which means the resolution of the eye is somewhat lower for lower light levels.

1.3 Visual Performance as a Function of Light Level

The human eye is faced with the formidable task of dealing with daytime and nighttime light levels that vary dramatically. Sunrise, sunset, and twilight definitions are used to establish generalizations with respect to the lighting levels associated with selected sun positions relative to the horizon. Sunset and sunrise are defined as the time at which the upper edge of the sun is on the visible horizon as seen from sea level with a clear horizon.[1] The angular radius of the sun is 16 arc minutes. There is a refractive effect (a bending of the light rays) by the atmosphere, due to the decrease in atmospheric density with altitude, such that the line of sight to the horizon actually curves downward so that we see slightly below the true horizon. Under typical conditions the angular displacement due to this refraction is 34 arc minutes. Combining these two effects, sunrise and sunset are defined as the times at which the center of the sun is 50 arc minutes below the horizon. *Civil twilight* is defined as the time at which the center of the sun is equal to or less than 6 degrees below the horizon. *Nautical twilight* is defined as the time at which the center of the sun is equal to or less than 12 degrees below the horizon and *astronomical twilight* is defined as the time at which the center of the sun is equal to or less than 18 degrees below the horizon. There are some historical descriptions of the three twilights. For example, "after the end of civil twilight, artificial illumination is normally required to carry on outdoor activities."[1] It is important that this loose definition not be taken to mean that we can see as well at the darkest region of civil twilight as we can during the daytime hours. That is certainly not true, as will be discussed later. In a similar fashion, nautical twilight obtained its name from the fact that the use of the sextant for navigational purposes was limited by the fact that the horizon is becoming "indistinct" at the darkest levels of nautical twilight. And light levels associated with the darkest levels of astronomical twilight are such as to not interfere with telescopic observations of terrestrial objects.

One generality that appears to be sparked by these twilight definitions is that headlights are required 30 minutes before and after sunset. This is a rough match to civil twilight. For example at 30 degrees latitude (San Diego is 32 degrees), civil twilight is 27 minutes before and after sunset on both December 21 (sun furthest south) and June 21 (sun furthest north), which is a pretty good approximation to the half-hour rule. However, at 60 degrees latitude (Anchorage is 61 degrees) civil twilight on December 21 is 58 minutes before and after sunset and on June 21 is 1 hour 47 minutes before and after sunset. So the half-hour headlight rule is not appropriate for Alaska.

Figure 1.1 shows the relationship between horizontal illumination and sun position.[2] It also shows the horizontal illumination generated by a full moon and a half moon as a function of the moon elevation.

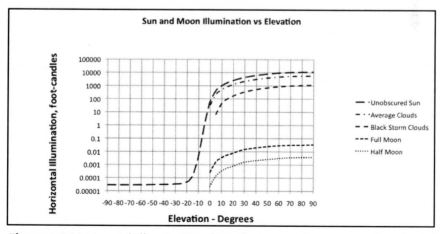

Figure 1.1 *Horizontal illumination from the sun and moon as a function of elevation angle.*

The horizontal illumination values in Figure 1.1 cover a range of more than one billion to one. Specific values of horizontal illumination for conditions of interest would include the following:

Condition	Elevation (Degrees)	Horizontal Illumination (Foot Candles)
Unobscured Sun		11,500
Average Clouds	90	5,750
Black Storm Clouds		1,150
Unobscured Sun		4,370
Average Clouds	30	2,185
Black Storm Clouds		437
Sunrise/set	-0.8	42
Civil Twilight	-6.0	0.32
Nautical Twilight	-12.0	0.0009
Astronomical Twilight	-18.0	0.00006
Full Moon Clear Sky	90	0.035
Full Moon Clear Sky	30	0.015
Half Moon Clear Sky	90	0.004
Half Moon Clear Sky	30	0.002

It is of particular interest to note that between sunset and the darkest portion of civil twilight the natural illumination drops by a factor of approximately 131 to 1. From the darkest portion of civil twilight to the darkest portion of nautical twilight the natural illumination drops by a factor of approximately 356 to 1. Therefore, from sunset to the darkest portion of nautical twilight, natural illumination drops by a factor of approximately 47,000 to 1. These are dramatic changes and have profound effect on our visual capabilities.

In analyzing the visibility issues in an accident, it is important to determine the natural lighting conditions that were involved. It is also important that any visit to the accident site for the purpose of investigating the accident visibility conditions be done at a date and time when reasonable duplication of the accident conditions exist. An important source of this kind of information is the United States Naval Observatory.[3] On this website you can enter a city, state (or a latitude and longitude), and a date to obtain the needed information. Various data options are available. These include a listing of the beginning and end of civil twilight, sunrise, sunset, moonrise, and moonset along with the percentage of the

Moon's visible disk. You can also obtain sun and moon azimuth and elevation data at selected time intervals for a complete day.

As mentioned in the preceding paragraph, the pupil of the eye expands at lower light levels. Pupil diameter ranges from about 2 millimeters at high light levels to approximately 8 millimeters at the lowest light levels. This 4 to 1 increase in pupil diameter results in a 16 to 1 increase in the area of the pupil and, therefore, in a 16 to 1 increase in light delivered to the receptor array. This falls far short of dealing with the dramatic change in the amount of light reaching the retina due to natural illumination at various times of day. The receptors do undergo an adaptation process in which the neural output per unit of input light energy falls off with increased light level. There is another technique used by the eye in dealing with this wide range of light levels. It involves the use of two types of receptors in the retina of the eye. They are called cones and rods. The cones are the primary receptors at higher light levels, that is, daylight operation. The cones are solely responsible for color vision. If you can see the color of an object, you are viewing it with your cones. The rods, on the other hand, are more efficient than the cones at lower light levels, capable of performing at light levels at which the cones supply no useful information. At higher light levels the rods are saturated and provide little output. Adaptation refers to the time interval involved in moving from one light level to another before full visual performance is regained. Light adaptation, that is, moving from the dark into the light, is a much faster process than dark adaptation. It has been the author's personal experience that the vast majority of accidents analyzed in terms of visibility issues, have involved light levels, combined natural and artificial lighting, at which there would have been primarily cone vision.

In the human retina near the center of the visual field is a region called the *central fovea*. The central fovea contains only cones. During daylight hours, the central fovea is the portion of the retina used for performing visual functions requiring high resolution, such as reading. The central fovea is roughly two degrees in angular size. That is about the angular size of a thumbnail held at arm's length. Moving away from the central fovea, there is an increase in the number of rod receptors with a corresponding decrease in the number of cone receptors. Figure 1.2 shows the distribution of cones and rods in the retina.[4] From Figure 1.2, the reader can see the dramatic decrease in the cone population and increase in the rod population moving away from the central fovea. Moving away from the central fovea there is also an increase in the size of the cones and the manner in which they are interconnected, which results in a decrease in resolution of fine detail. There are other changes in receptor properties in the periphery, most notable of which is that some peripheral receptors have an increased sensitivity to motion. Sensing peripheral motion is generally followed by a movement of our eyes to point them in the direction of the movement in order to view the source of the motion with our central fovea.

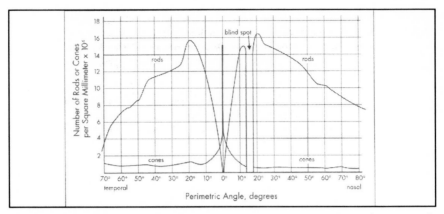

Figure 1.2 Density of rods and cones in the human retina as a function of peripheral angle.

1.4 Central Fovea Resolution

The size of the individual receptors in the retina and the resolving power of the lens system of the eye both contribute to determining the visual resolution, which is the extent to which we can see fine detail. From a "design" perspective, it is not surprising that the size of the cones in the central fovea and the resolving power of the lens are well matched. The reading of the letters on an eye chart is perhaps the most familiar demonstration of resolution. When viewed at a distance of 20 feet, the letters on the "20/20" line are somewhat fuzzy but recognizable for an individual with "normal" vision. The height and width of these letters are such that they subtend an angle of five arc minutes (an arc minute is 1/60 of a degree). On the eye chart the letter height on the "20/20" line is roughly $^3/_8$ of an inch. You can visualize the letter "E" as consisting of five separate intervals in the vertical dimension. Vertically, there is a bar, a space, a bar, a space, and a bar. Therefore, each of these stroke widths is $^1/_5$ the total five arc minutes, or one arc minute of angle. This is the level of detail that must be recognized in order to clearly distinguish one letter from another. It is sometimes useful to associate an eye chart with a visual task related to an accident. For example, if we were to create an eye chart for use at 300 feet instead of 20 feet, the letters would have to be 15 times higher or a little over 5 inches. This can be of assistance in visualizing the level of detail that it is possible to discern at that distance. It should be noted that visual acuity does decrease as the scene light level decreases.

1.5 Daytime Peripheral Resolution

As shown in Figure 1.2, the number of cones per unit area decreases rapidly from the central fovea out into the periphery. That being the case, it is apparent that resolution will also decrease. For an individual with 20/20 vision, visual acuity 10 degrees off axis (approximately the width of a hand held at arm's length) will be on the order of 20/100. At 20 degrees off axis the visual acuity will drop to something on the order of 20/200, which happens to be the definition of legally blind. Therefore, while our peripheral vision is very valuable, it is no substitute for the central fovea when it comes to seeing detail. As a simple experiment, fixate on the left hand margin of this page and, without moving your eyes, determine what you are able to recognize in terms of words or letters on the right hand edge of the page. Visual search frequently involves a sequence of events which may start with peripheral "detection" (something is present), followed by eye movement to place that "something" on the central fovea after which "recognition" takes place (determination as to the general type of object, for example, a person), and, with additional mental processing, "identification" is accomplished (the person is John Smith).

1.6 Photometric Quantities

It is necessary to define some terms used in the measurement of light in order to give meaning to visual performance. Light is propagated in the form of waves of electromagnetic energy, like a radio wave but of much higher frequency. When we deal with just those frequencies of radiation to which the eye is sensitive, that is, the visible spectrum, we use a system of units that measures the energy in terms of its effectiveness in producing a visual stimulus. A *lumen* is a unit of visible light power analogous to the watt. The product of lumens and time (e.g., lumen-seconds) is a measure of energy, analogous to watt-seconds or watt-hours. Power density is a measure of the amount of power in a spatial area. For example, if we were measuring the power density received from a radio tower we could talk about the number of watts received per square foot of receiving area (watts per square foot). In a corresponding manner, the power density received from a light source can be measured in terms of the number of lumens received per square foot of receiving surface (lumens per square foot), which is the definition of a *foot-candle*, abbreviated as *fc*. The metric equivalent is the lux (lumens per square meter). We refer to this as illumination. When light falls on a diffuse surface, that is, one that reflects light uniformly in all directions (not shiny), and we look at that surface, we have a sensation of *brightness*. The appropriate photometric term is *luminance*. Luminance is a scientifically defined lighting parameter that can be measured with a light meter. Brightness is the mental sensation generated by viewing an object. Figure 1.3 illustrates the distinction between luminance and brightness. In this digital image, the two circles have equal digital values. If you use a light meter and measure the luminance of each circle you will find they are identical. However, our eyes see the circle on

Figure 1.3 *Perceived brightness of a circular target for different background luminance.*

the left as "brighter" than the circle on the right. This is due to the difference in background for the two circles.

The common unit of measurement of luminance is the *foot Lambert*, abbreviated as *fL*. The luminance of a diffuse surface is equal to the number of foot-candles of illumination falling on the surface multiplied by the *reflectance* of the surface. The contrast, C, of an object with respect to its background is defined as the luminance of the object or target, B_T, minus the luminance of the background, B_B, that quantity divided by the luminance of the background, B_B.

$$C = (B_T - B_B) / B_B \qquad\qquad \text{Eq 1.1}$$

Contrast is dimensionless. A black object viewed against a non-black background has a contrast of

$$C = (0 - B_B) B_B = -1 \qquad\qquad \text{Eq 1.2}$$

Whereas, an object twice the luminance of the background has a contrast of,

$$C = (2B_B - B_B) / B_B = +1. \qquad\qquad \text{Eq 1.3}$$

So objects, darker than the background, have contrasts that are a negative value, with a maximum value of -1, whereas objects of luminance greater than the background against which they are viewed have positive contrast. Positive contrast can be very large numbers, as for example, a headlamp viewed against a very dark background. This definition of contrast, called *universal contrast*, was adopted because experiments have shown that, using this definition, negative and positive contrasts of the same numerical value are approximately equally detectable. For example a black object viewed against a specific background has approximately the same detectability as an object with twice the luminance of the background.

1.7 Visual Detection Performance

There are a number of laboratories that have devoted substantial effort to the generation of data defining the capabilities and limitations of the human visual system. Extensive vision experiments were conducted during World War II at the Tiffany Foundation.[5] This research produced a large body of contrast threshold data. Other laboratories that have contributed to the generation of this data include the University of Michigan Research Institute, the Visibility Laboratory, Scripps Institution of Oceanography, University of California, and the Institute for Research in Vision, Ohio State University. These research laboratories performed visual *detection* experiments, where detection implies the capability for an observer to determine that *something* is present as differentiated from *recognition* or *identification*, each of which implies higher levels of awareness as to the nature of the target. The primary variables that determine the level of difficulty of detection of a visual target are angular size, contrast, time available for observation, adaptation luminance level, and retinal position within the visual field of view. Angular size has been previously discussed. With respect to time available for observation, a wide variety of stimulus presentation times were used in these experiments. In some of this research, emphasis was placed on times of $1/3$-second because that is the approximate duration of a typical fixation of the eye while performing visual search. Contrast threshold is the contrast required to make an object detectable at a specified probability. It is of no surprise that as the overall luminance level of a scene is reduced, the contrast thresholds of visual targets will increase.

To understand the significance of vision data it is helpful to understand the nature of a typical visual threshold experiment. Picture a group of observers seated viewing a large screen. Each observer has a set of response buttons. The screen is illuminated to a desired adaptation level. One type of experiment that has been frequently used involves the projection of circular targets onto the screen following an alerting buzzer. The observer would push a designated response button if the target is detected. The variables of the experiment would be the background luminance, the angular size of the target, the contrast of the target relative to its background, and/or the duration of the time interval during which the target is displayed. It is important to understand that the results of such an experiment will not be a single number for any of the variables involved. For a number of reasons, the results of any such experiment will be a rather broad distribution of data. At a fundamental level, light itself is statistical in nature. What we think of as a "steady stream" of light actually consists of discrete packets of energy called photons. Photons exhibit random properties such that during a specified series of equal time intervals, there will not be an equal number of photon arrivals. Another reason for the spread of experimental results is that there will be differences between observers, even with individuals receiving identical scores on an eye chart test. As targets are made more difficult to detect, "personality" differences will surface. Some observers will be more cautious than others in declaring that they see the target as they near threshold. For all observers, there will be "false positives" in which they respond that they have seen the target, even when the target is not presented. Furthermore, the observers can be manipulated as to the number of "false positives." For example, if you instruct observers that they will be paid $10 for every target they see and report, but that $1 will be deducted for every false positive they report, the observer will tend to "see" a lot of targets. On the other hand if you tell the observers that they will be paid $1 for every target they see and report but that $10 will be deducted for every false positive they report, they will become very cautious. Also, if you lead the observer to believe that the targets are "always" present, the number of false targets reported will increase. These same factors can also come into play for observations made by an expert at an accident site. For example, suppose there is a question as to how far away a parked automobile without lights can be seen. When an expert parks an automobile at the accident scene and then backs away to determine the maximum sighting distance, he does so knowing full well that the vehicle is there and this will tend to bias his observation. This is one way in which *expectation* factors into visual sightings.

To take personality and expectation out of vision experiments, a procedure known as *forced choice* is frequently used. A typical forced choice experiment would consist of using a buzzer to mark off four time intervals with the target being displayed during one of these four time intervals, with the selected time interval chosen at random. The observer is given a set of four response buttons and the response is in terms of which of the four intervals contained the target. As the contrast of the target is lowered, a point will be reached where the data shows the correct response is obtained 25 percent of the time, that is, the observer is guessing. As the contrast of the target is increased, the probability of correct decision will increase until the contrast is of such a value that the probability reaches 100 percent. *Liminal contrast* is defined as the contrast that produces 50 percent correct response.

For the reasons discussed above and others associated with visual search, the distance at which an object can be sighted is not a single number but rather a distribution of numbers. When we discuss whether an individual could have or should have seen an object we are forced to deal with a probability distribution and we can only realistically discuss performance in terms of percentiles, as, for example, 85 percent of the population would be able to see the object at this distance. Caution is required when assessing fault based on percentile numbers. For example, if an 85 percent number is used as a basis for assessing fault, 15 percent of the population will be assigned fault even though they may have done nothing wrong.

1.8 Numerical Examples of Visual Detection Threshold Data

As previously stated, the important factors determining the detectability of a target are the scene luminance level, contrast, angular size, and location of the target within the visual field of view. Blackwell and Taylor published experimental data relating *detection threshold contrast* as a function of background luminance and peripheral location (degrees from center of fovea).[6] One of the many experiments they report involved a stimulus time of 1/100 second, and a target size of 0.776 arc minutes. Since the resolution of the eye is approximately 1 arc minute, retinal images of targets subtending an angle less than 1 arc minute will have little change in shape but will simply appear less bright as the angular size is reduced. In Figure 1.4, which shows a sample of this experimental data, the contrast threshold data has been normalized to a value of 1 for a background

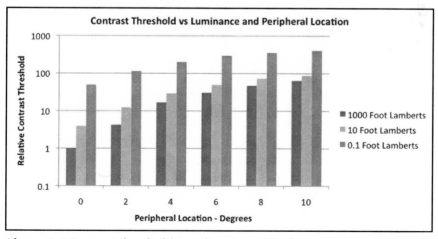

Figure 1.4 *Contrast threshold as a function of background luminance and peripheral location.*

luminance of 1000 foot Lamberts with the target located at the center of the fovea in order to make it easier to visualize the range of numerical values involved.

Because of the large range of the numbers involved, it was necessary to use a logarithmic scale in order to show the relative contrast threshold values. The numerical values for the chart are as follows:

Background Luminance (Foot Lamberts)	Target Off-Axis (Degrees)	Relative Detection (Contrast Threshold)
1000	0	1.0
	2	4.2
	4	16.6
	6	30.6
	8	47.5
	10	64.5
10	0	3.9
	2	12.2
	4	29.3
	6	49.6
	8	73.6
	10	87.7
0.1	0	49.6
	2	114.1
	4	201.7
	6	299.4
	8	356.8
	10	406.9

Keep in mind that this data is for the case of small angular size targets (unresolved). This data points out the profound effect that scene luminance level and peripheral location have upon target detectability. In an attempt to aid in the interpretation of this data, consider the following. Midday on a sunny day may produce background luminance levels of 1000 foot Lamberts. Sunset on a mid-summer clear day provides a horizontal illumination of approximately 42 foot-candles. With a pavement reflectance of about 30 percent, the pavement luminance is about 10 foot Lamberts. The chart shows that over the daylight range of luminance (1000 to 10 foot Lamberts), for direct foveal fixation (0 degrees off-axis), there is an increase of approximately 4 to 1 in terms of contrast threshold. Under these same conditions, the same roadway would have a luminance of approximately 0.1 foot Lamberts at civil twilight (roughly one-half hour after sunset—headlights required), and the chart shows that objects need to have about 50 times as much contrast to be detected with direct foveal fixation. So while we may feel that we are seeing well one-half hour after sunset, our visual capabilities have been substantially reduced when compared with those at midday.

With respect to peripheral vision, this data shows that during broad daylight (1000 foot-Lamberts), a target located 10 degrees off-axis will require 65 times as much contrast in order to be detected as compared with a target on which we are fixated. In the neighborhood of civil twilight (0.1 foot-candles—one-half hour after sunset) a target located 10 degrees off-axis will require over 400 times as much contrast in order to be detected, as compared with a target on which we are fixated (0 degrees off-axis) during 1000 foot-Lamberts, broad daylight, conditions, and roughly eight times as much contrast as for the case of direct foveal viewing of the target under 0.1 foot Lambert conditions. It is hoped that these examples will assist in making it clear that there are serious limitations to peripheral vision and, specifically, underscore the importance of taking these limitations into consideration when visiting an accident site under conditions in which we know exactly where we need to look to see the target of interest.

To illustrate the effect of angular target size on *contrast threshold*, numerical results from a set of experiments performed by Dr. John Taylor at the Visibility Laboratory will be referenced.[7] These tests involved a forced choice experiment in which circular targets were projected with a background luminance of 75 foot Lamberts, and a projection time of 0.33 seconds. The time was chosen because this is the typical time involved in a single visual fixation. The targets were projected onto the center of the screen so that viewing would be with the central fovea. The experiment was designed to determine the liminal threshold (50 percent correct observer response) as a function of the angular size of the target. For purposes of the chart that follows, the contrast threshold values are normalized to a value of 1.0 for an angular diameter of 0.5 arc minutes. Sample results from the experiment are shown in Figure 1.5. The following are the numerical values from Figure 1.5:

Target Diameter (Arc Minutes)	Liminal (Threshold Contrast)
0.5	0.985
1.00	0.233
10.2	0.014
120.0	0.007

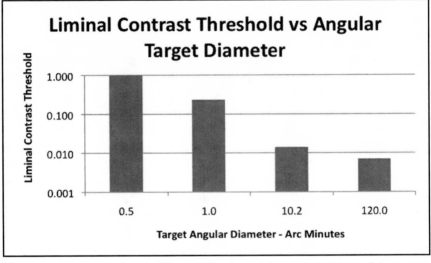

Figure 1.5 *Contrast threshold as a function of the angular size of the target.*

It is of interest to note that 0.5 arc minutes is below the 1 arc minute resolution of the human eye. The retinal image of an unresolved circular target will not change in shape with increase or decrease of target angular size; instead the total light energy in the image will be proportional to the area of the target. Thus a 2 to 1 change in the diameter of the target (4 to 1 change in area) will produce a 4 to 1 change in the threshold contrast. As the target diameter is increased to extend into the "resolved target" region, the decrease in threshold contrast with increase in target angular diameter shows a change less than the change in target area, as for example the change in target diameter from 1.00 to 10.2 (approximately 100 to 1 in target area) that results in a decrease in threshold contrast by a factor of only approximately 17 to 1. With further increase in target size, the reduction in contrast threshold decreases substantially. For example, a change in target size from 10.2 arc minutes to 120 arc minutes (138 to 1 change in target area) results in a contrast threshold decrease by a factor of only 2 to 1.

The following equation is a good fit to this particular experimental data (B = 75 foot Lamberts, T = 0.33 seconds):

$$\text{Liminal Contrast Threshold} = 0.24/\text{alpha}^2 + 0.025/\text{alpha} + 0.0075 \qquad \text{Eq. 1.4}$$

where alpha is the angular diameter of the target in arc minutes. The first of the three terms represents the unresolved target, the second term represents the resolved target, and the final term represents the situation when the target diameter reaches a level such that further increases in target diameter do not result in a decrease in contrast threshold.

1.9 Visual Search

As previously discussed, during daylight hours, the central fovea is required for seeing detail or detecting small objects. Visual search is the process of pointing the eyes in different directions to accomplish this task. Studies have shown that in performing such search the eye makes very rapid movements followed by a stationary period on the order of $1/3$-second. With this type of search, detection is accomplished during the stationary period and not during the rapid eye movement. All of us carry in our minds, often unconsciously, a priority list as to what we believe is important in the world around us. The priority list forms the basis for the pointing of our eyes. The extent to which a driver looks to her right or left will depend upon the circumstances. A driver approaching an intersection is an obvious example. When conclusions are drawn as to whether a particular object should have been seen in time to prevent an accident, visual search needs to be considered. There have been studies made as to the visual search that is carried out by the driver of an automobile under various conditions.[8] It is perfectly normal, in fact desirable, that drivers occasionally look to their right, to their left, in their rear view mirror, at their speedometer, and so on. Less desirable visual distraction would include radios, cell phones, maps, lunch, and so on. The referenced study indicted that, at night, on a non-illuminated highway, a driver may be looking directly forward approximately 75 percent of the time. Obviously, the time at which a target is first detected will be later if the driver was not looking in that direction when the target first appeared. It is not expected that a driver will spend long periods of time looking away from the direction of travel, but even a one second glance can have large significance in terms of the time at which visual acquisition is accomplished. It is also important to recognize that when two objects approach on a collision course, the direction in which each party must look to see the other is dependent upon the speeds of each, but may well be significantly away from the direction of travel and therefore scan patterns and peripheral vision characteristics must be used in evaluating whether each party should have seen the other. For example, assume we have a collision encounter such that the driver would need to look 30 degrees to the left to see the collision threat. If the driver is spending 75 percent of the time looking directly forward, that leaves only 25 percent of the time to look in all other directions. If looking left and looking right are equally valid actions then that would suggest that the time spent looking to the left would be less than 12.5 percent. That being the case, the likelihood that the driver will be looking in the direction of the conflict target is small, and these factors must be considered when determining a driver's ability to see a target.

1.10 Application of Detection Threshold Experiments to Real World Situations

The detection contrast threshold experiments that have been described provide useful insight into the capabilities of the human visual system. Unfortunately, there are some serious limitations with respect to the direct application of this data to accident situations for the purpose of calculating the distance at which visual target acquisition will take place. Several examples of these limitations are given in the following sections.

1.11 Non-circular and Non-uniform Luminance Targets

There are some accident visibility issues which can be addressed using the contrast threshold data to calculate the distance associated with visual sightings. One example is the calculation of the distance at which a taillight or brakelight can be visually detected. Here the "target" may be basically circular with uniform luminance viewed against a reasonably uniform luminance background, and the experimental data is a good fit to the situation at hand. However, there are many situations is which the target is not circular with non-uniform luminance. The detectability of this type of target has not been adequately determined. One consideration is the extent to which the visual system uses variations in target luminance, such as edge detection, to enhance detectability. Provided herein are a few simple examples to illustrate this issue. Figure 1.6 contains two circular targets, the left one blurred on the outer edge. The left circle visually appears to have a reduced contrast and is therefore less detectable. Both of the circles shown have the same digital values in the central portion of the image, but the edges of the left circle are blurred. Figure 1.7 shows the same image with the blurred edge removed from the left circle. Now the two circles appear to have the same contrast. In Figure 1.8 there are three circular, uniform luminance targets, and the same three circles on the left with the center removed to form a donut shape. The three "donut" images appear to be at least as detectable, if not more detectable than the original circular target. This suggests that the area of the target is not the defining factor. It is interesting to note that if edge detection is indeed an important factor then, for a circular target, the amount of "edge" is proportional to the circumference (pi times the diameter) of the circle, which is in agreement with the experimental finding that, for resolved circular targets, detectability is more nearly proportional to target circumference rather than to target area.

If "edge detection" plays a major role in determining the visibility of an object, there is an important implication related to human visual capability. That is because any reduction in visual acuity from the "normal" 20/20 means an increased blurring in the edge detail of the images of objects, and therefore a decrease in detectability. The implication is that reduced visual acuity can reduce

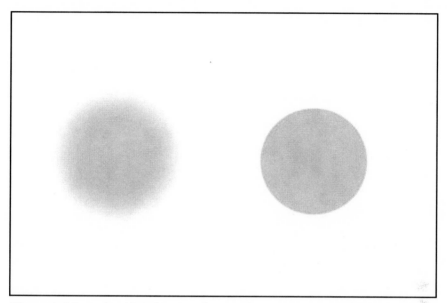

Figure 1.6 *Perceived brightness of a circular target as a function of edge sharpness.*

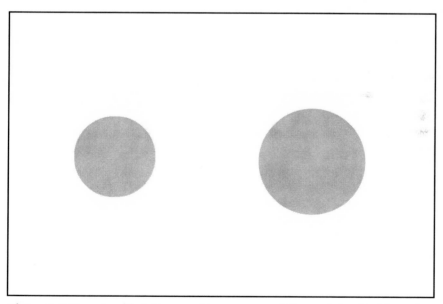

Figure 1.7 *Perceived brightness of two targets of Figure 1.6 with blurred edge removed from the left hand circle.*

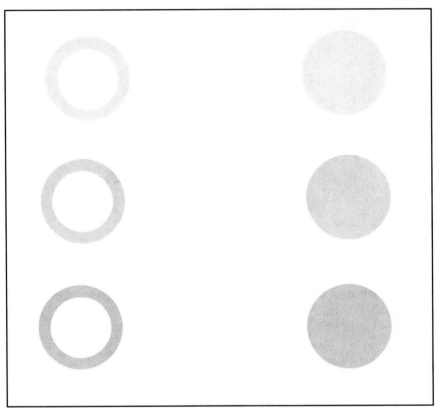

Figure 1.8 *Perceived brightness of three circular targets with and without central region removed.*

the detectability of large targets as well as small targets. This suggests that, when we have an accident involving an individual with reduced visual acuity, it may be useful to demonstrate the edge detection effect. One way of doing this is to take scene photos and subject them to resolution reduction (blurring) consistent with the visual acuity of an individual involved in the accident in order to allow visualization of the extent to which reduced visual acuity may affect the ability to extract important information from the scene. There could be cases in which visual acuity might need to be considered in the selection of the jury.

1.12 Visual Search with Complex Backgrounds

As previously mentioned, *detection* involves sensing that "something" is there, as differentiated from *recognition* or *identification* which both require some level of differentiation as to the nature of the "something." Related to visibility issues in accidents, there are situations in which a low level of recognition may be all that is required. For example, suppose a driver sees that there is an object of some kind lying in the roadway in the intended path of travel. Depending upon the circumstances, this may be sufficient information to allow a driver to consider alternatives to avoid striking the object, that is, braking or changing lanes. A pilot, facing a uniform sky background, sees "something" in the sky in his peripheral vision. Anything in the sky poses a potential threat to a pilot. Sighting "something" with peripheral vision will cause the pilot to point his eyes directly at the object. With a uniform field of view, such as the sky, peripheral detection, followed by eye movements to place the object in the central fovea, may work very well.

There are times, however, when meaningful visual acquisition requires higher levels of visual discrimination. For example, assume that a driver is rounding a curve on a residential roadway. Objects ahead may include trees, bushes, fence posts, mailboxes and, perhaps, a pedestrian. Under these circumstances, it is of vital importance that the driver be able to distinguish between these alternative objects. Peripheral vision has limited value under circumstances where the background includes lots of "somethings" because peripheral vision does not have the capability to resolve fine detail. This means we have to look directly at each "something" to see if it is of interest, which dramatically slows the visual search process. Figures 1.9 and 1.10 are simple examples to illustrate the problem.

In Figure 1.9, assume that you are asked to find the letter "U" on the page. You can fixate virtually anywhere on the page and detect the presence of "something." You will now fixate on the "something" and immediately recognize it as the letter "U." In Figure 1.10, assume that you are asked to find the letter "Q." In this case, peripheral vision will not allow us to make such a ready identification. It is necessary to perform a visual search of the page, fixating close enough on each letter to allow foveal inspection and identification of the letter. The time required to perform this task is going to be substantially greater than for a single object located on a uniform background. In situations with limited time available to respond and a large number of background objects to be identified, the likelihood of detecting and identifying some important element in the scene will be dramatically reduced and, in fact, may not occur.

Backgrounds are not just simple or complex but rather have levels of complexity. The measure of complexity is the extent to which elements of the background resemble objects of interest when viewed with the resolution associated with peripheral vision.[9] The other factor which needs to be taken into consideration is that the human visual system tends to be single channeled, meaning that we mentally process one object image at a time. *Tunnel vision* is a term often used in a derogatory fashion but it is, in fact, an accurate description of the way in which the human visual system often performs. For example, if the driver

Figure 1.9 Visual detection and identification of a single letter on a uniform background.

Figure 1.10 Visual detection and identification of a single letter in the presence of multiple letters on a uniform background.

of an automobile sees another oncoming automobile and believes that vehicle poses a threat, full attention will be devoted to that automobile causing a pedestrian within the driver's field of view to go unseen, even though under normal circumstances the pedestrian might be clearly visible. This is in keeping with the concept of establishing priorities and using them as a basis for apportioning our time and effort. It is "playing the odds."

Perception-reaction time is generally described as the time interval between the detection of a visual stimulus and the initiation of an action based upon the interpretation of that visual stimulus. A simple example is the time interval between the appearance of the brake lights on the car that you are following and the time that your foot touches the brake pedal to initiate a slowing. In the reconstruction literature it is often treated as if it were a fundamental constant and given a value of 1.5 seconds[10] with arguments that under some conditions such as darkness and/or an unexpected event, it may rise to 2.5 seconds or higher.[11] Many published documents have suggested that even in the simplest of cases, with a hazard that is easily seen and appears essentially in front of the driver, perception-reaction time at the 85th percentile may be about 1.5 seconds. The validity of such assumed values is discussed in Chapter 3.[12] It has also been reported that with complications such as if the hazard is more difficult to detect, initially appears off to the side, or cannot readily be identified, perception-reaction time will be lengthened. How much longer is, at present, a matter of judgment. The person with the shortest perception-reaction time does not necessarily get first prize. That award goes to the individual who correctly interprets the situation and makes a good decision as to the proper course of action. As a dramatic example, the author has studied midair collisions in which a pilot responded to an encounter with another aircraft before he was able to make an accurate assessment of the situation and performed a maneuver that turned a "near-miss" into a collision.

1.13 Eyewitness Testimony

The testimony of participants in and witnesses to an accident can play a dominant role in the evidence presented at trial. Serious limitations in the accuracy of such testimony are discussed in Chapter 3.

1.14 Summary

My hope would be that the numerical information provided with respect to the performance capabilities and limitations of the human visual system would make the reader aware of the need to take these characteristics into consideration when attempting to draw conclusions as to whether parties involved in an accident could have or should have been able to take the necessary action to avoid the accident, based on the information they collect from visual observation. This would include recognizing the dramatic changes that take place in visual performance with reductions in light level, the contrast and angular size of objects of interest, and the limitations of visual capabilities associated with peripheral vision. It is extremely important that those of us who participate in accident investigations recognize that, when we go to an accident site, we are aware of what happened and we know exactly where the parties involved should have been fixating and what they should have been looking for in order to see and avoid the accident, whereas the parties involved in the accident did not have the benefit of this information. So in evaluating the visibility issues, we need to make the effort to take into consideration where the involved parties may have been fixating, given their mental priority list, generated in the absence of any knowledge of the upcoming accident.

One might expect that all of this experimental data defining human visual performance capability would allow easy calculations of the distances at which visual detection would take place in various types of accidents. Unfortunately, it is not that simple. The vision experiments providing this data involved the detection of uniformly illuminated circular targets located on a uniform background. It is not surprising that most accidents do not incorporate these important conditions. Many targets of interest in accidents have complex shape, non-uniform luminance, and are viewed against complex backgrounds. So while this data is extremely helpful in making us aware of the capabilities and limitations of the human visual system, it does not lend itself to the generation of numerical evaluation of visual performance in most accidents. It is for this reason that photographs, properly taken and displayed, as will be discussed in Chapter 2, are a valuable way of attempting to demonstrate the level of difficulty associated with the visual tasks associated with accidents.

Endnotes

1.   The Nautical Almanac, Department of the Navy, U.S. Naval Observatory.

2.   http://www.usno.navy.mil/USNO/astronomical-applications/data-services/data-services.

3.   Biberman, L. M., Lawrence Dunkelman, Marion Fickett, and Reinald Finke, "Levels of Nocturnal Illumination," Institute for Defense Analysis, Research Paper P-232, January 1966.

4.   Lighting Handbook, Eighth Edition, Illuminating Engineering Society of North America, 1993, Pg 72.

5.   Blackwell, H. R. "Contrast thresholds of the human eye." JOSA 36: 624-643, 1946.

6.   H. Richard Blackwell, John H. Taylor "Survey of Laboratory Studies of Visual Perception," North Atlantic Treaty Organization Seminar on "Detection, Recognition, and Identification of Line-of-Sight Targets," The Hague, Netherlands, 25-29 August 1969.

7.   Taylor, John H., Applied Optics, May 1964, pp. 562-569

8.   Driver Search and Scan Patterns in Night Driving, Nick J. Rachoff, Pennsylvania State University and Thomas H. Rockwell, The Ohio State University, Symposium Paper, "Driver Visual Needs in Night Driving," September 4-6, 1974 at Ohio State University, conducted by Transportation Research Board and sponsored by Illuminating Research Institute, Ohio State University and Ohio Department of Transportation.

9.   "A Possible Criterion for Visual Recognition Thresholds," J. L. Harris. Scripps Institution of Oceanography, SIO 59-65, Nov 1959.

10. "Accident Reconstruction," James C. Collins, Charles C. Thomas Publisher, 1979

11. "A Policy on Geometric Design of Highways and Streets" 1984, American Association of State Highway and Transportation Officials.

12. Olson, Paul L., Robert Dewar and Eugene Farber. *Forensic Aspects of Driver Perception and Response, Third Edition*. Lawyers & Judges Publishing, 2010.

Chapter 2

Forensic Photography

2.1 Introduction

There are many reasons for the use of photography at an accident scene. One of great importance would be documenting information related to physical evidence, for example, vehicle damage, gouge and skid marks, and so on. Photographs taken for this purpose have no requirement for duplicating the lighting conditions at the time of the accident and may well be taken using headlights or a camera flash to help illuminate the evidence of interest.

With respect to visibility issues, there is no question that photographs can be extremely valuable. People viewing a picture will form strong opinions with respect to whether objects in the scene are easy or difficult to see. The critical question is, will these opinions be correct? A picture that does not accurately depict the scene, as the participants in the accident would have viewed it, can result in false impressions regarding visibility. The conditions required to produce accurate representations of a scene are discussed below.[1] It is important to understand that the objective of such photographs is not to "simulate the human visual system" but simply to replicate the scene. If the overall process is performed properly, the person viewing the final product will insert the characteristics of the human visual system.

There is one other factor to be considered. Assume that the objective is to show the jury that a "target" of interest, even though of low contrast, would have been visible. If the scene is displayed with fidelity, the impression formed by each jury member may well depend upon their own visual capabilities and limitations, so the jury selection process might need to include questions in this regard.

The author has a limited role with respect to photography. The advice herein is not for artistic photography. The author's knowledge and skill with respect to photography are limited to the technical aspects of generating realistic representations of how an accident scene would have appeared to the parties involved.

2.2 Scene Fidelity

If pictures are taken to demonstrate the level of difficulty associated with critical visibility issues, it is essential that the accident scene be realistically duplicated. This would include coordinating the position of the sun and moon to be substantially the same for the accident date and time as the the picture date and time. Weather conditions, cloud cover and visibility need to be considered. In terms of artificial illumination, it is important to know if there have been any changes to the light sources in the area. Wet pavement can dramatically alter the visibility of scene objects. If headlight or taillight illumination is involved then there needs to be a reasonable duplication of vehicle types. To demonstrate a driver's visibility capabilities, photos need to be taken from a position in the vehicle similar to that of the eye position of the driver. In pedestrian accidents, an exemplar with similar clothing (color and reflectance) needs to be employed. The camera flash unit can be very useful in documenting physical evidence at the scene but cannot be used when the objective is to address visibility issues.

Figure 2.1 is a photo taken using the camera flash. Figure 2.2 is a photo of the same scene without the flash. Both photos were taken with the camera set on "automatic exposure."

For low light levels, the flash adds substantial light to the nearby portions of the scene, and this results in a large reduction in the exposure settings. The flash illumination decreases with the square of the distance so that more distant portions of the scene will receive no significant illumination. With the reduced

Figure 2.1 *Photograph of a scene with flash.*

Figure 2.2 *Photograph of the same scene without flash.*

exposure settings, the more distant objects will appear to be much darker than shown in the photograph taken without flash, and therefore with increased exposure settings. The flash has dramatically altered the apparent visibility of objects in the scene. It should also be noted that the use of a flash will exaggerate the luminance of any retroreflective materials in the scene.

2.3 Photographic Fidelity

The camera taking the pictures and the devices used to display the results need to have a resolution that is either equal to or somewhat better than the human eye so that the level of fine detail available to the viewer is determined by the eye of the observer of the photograph and not by the equipment used to take and display the photographs. The basic factors that determine the visibility of an object include the angular size of objects in the scene, the contrast of the object with respect to the background against which it is viewed, and the light level of the scene.

2.4 Viewing Distance

For every photograph there is only one viewing distance at which objects in the photograph will have the same angular size as they would appear at the scene. This is determined by matching the angular size of the viewed image to the angular field of view of the lens used to take the photograph. The camera used in this instance has a sensor that is 36×24mm, which is a size match to 35mm film. With a 50mm lens, the ratio of the lens focal length to the horizontal dimensions of the image sensor is approximately 1.39 to 1. To achieve angular fidelity with the 50mm lens, the eyes of the observer need to be located at a distance of 1.39 times the width of the image being viewed. For a paper print 10 inches wide, that would mean the proper viewing distance is 13.9 inches. For an image filling a 5 foot wide projection screen that would mean the viewing distance should be approximately 7 feet; for a 10 foot wide screen, approximately 14 feet. For courtroom presentation it is important to take into consideration the geometry associated with the jury box and plausible screen and projector locations. To achieve a practical viewing distance, image cropping can be a useful tool. For example, a 50mm lens produces a horizontal field of view of approximately 40 degrees. If the scene detail of interest can be limited to 20 degrees then the viewing distances can be increased to 2.83 times the horizontal dimensions of the projected image. Additional considerations associated with the use of cropping include achieving a better match of photo and projector resolution limits as will be discussed in Section 2.6, *Digital Camera Resolution.*

2.5 Camera Types

Over the years, there has been a dramatic increase in the use of digital cameras as compared with traditional film cameras. The authors have joined this movement. There have been complaints that digital photographs can be easily manipulated and therefore should not be allowed in the courtroom due to the false impression they may make regarding visibility. This claim will be discussed in the paragraphs that follow.

Let us start with a very brief word about film cameras, in which a picture is taken by exposing negative film, which is then processed and printed to produce the final product. There are a large number of film types, processing chemicals and papers on the market. Suffice it to say that it is entirely possible to choose a combination of films, chemicals, processing times, procedures, and papers to produce a final product in which the contrast and luminance (brightness) of objects in the scene are incorrectly displayed. The author has heard trial testimony in which a laboratory technician stated that he was asked to reprocess and print pictures (lighter or darker, more or less contrast) to achieve an end product more beneficial to the "cause." If end product fidelity is a matter of importance, cross-examination of a photographer that has produced prints using a conventional film camera would have to involve questions that would include, not only the film type and the camera settings, but the film processing chemicals used, its strength, the processing time, the printing paper (including its contrast rating), the enlarger light level and exposure time, and the developing chemicals and times used to generate the prints, followed by testimony from a photographic expert capable of explaining what all of this means in terms of the end product fidelity.

Digital photographs, on the other hand, can indeed be "manipulated" to produce final images having characteristics more favorable to one side or the other. For the same reasons, digital cameras offer a better opportunity to use the available processing techniques to create end product pictures that are more accurate representations of the depicted scenes. Attorneys must become more knowledgeable of digital cameras and digital processing so that they can adequately cross-examine photographers who have recorded images using a digital camera to determine the accuracy of the end product. This section of this book is useful in this regard. When a digital camera product is used to demonstrate visibility, the original image, which has not been subjected to any type of modification, should be recorded and made available to all interested parties. This recording should include all of the information related to date, time, lens aperture settings, shutter time, and ISO settings. ISO settings are provided by the International Organization for Standardization. In a digital camera they are a measure of sensitivity. This will be discussed in more detail throughout this chapter. All of this information is commonly imbedded in digital form with each image.

2.6 Digital Camera Resolution

There are a number of factors that determine the resolution of a recorded image. The following is a brief description of these items. In a digital camera, the lens forms an image of the scene on a detector array consisting of discreet photosensitive detector elements. The resolution is described in terms of the size of the pixel array, usually advertised in terms of the total number of pixels. For example, an array having 2000 pixels horizontally by 1500 pixels vertically would be described as 3 megapixels (3,000,000 pixels). To achieve fidelity, it is necessary to capture a scene with somewhat better resolution than that of the human eye in order that the resolution experienced by the viewer of the scene will be limited in seeing fine detail by the resolution of the eyes of the viewers and not by the resolution of the camera. One way of demonstrating the image resolution is to photograph a conventional eye chart at a distance of 20 feet. By looking at the eye chart image, the camera resolution relative to human vision can be observed. Figure 2.3 is a pair of photos taken at a distance of 20 feet with a 50mm lens set at f/16. A 50mm lens with a 36×24mm image detector array covers a horizontal field of view of approximately 40 degrees. The resolution of the human eye is approximately 1 arc minute. Therefore a pixel array of 60×40 = 2400 pixels would make each pixel correspond to a resolution of 1 arc minute. The eye chart on the left was taken with the camera resolution set to 2250×1500 pixels and the right eye chart with an array size of 4500×3000 pixels. Line 8 is the 20/20 line on the eye chart. In the left eye chart, on the 20/20 line, the letters are a little blurry but recognizable. In the right eye chart, with 4500×3000 pixel resolution, the 20/20 line letters are easily identified. Line 9 is the 20/15 line, line 10 is 20/13, and line 11 is 20/10. The important point is that a 50mm lens on a camera with a 36×24mm image sensor array will produce images with a resolution somewhat better than the human visual system so that the resolution will be determined by the eye of the observer and not by the camera. A longer focal length lens can be used to reduce the pixel requirement. For example an 85mm lens with a 36×24mm image sensor array covers a field of view of approximately 24 degrees. To make each pixel correspond to 1 arc minute resolution would require 60×24 = 1440 pixels horizontally. To insure that the final resolution is determined by the eye of the observer and not by the camera, a horizontal pixel count on the order of 2880 would satisfy the requirement.

2.7 Exposure Options

The quantity of light energy that reaches a single pixel in the detector array of the camera is proportional to the luminance of the scene associated with that pixel, the area of the lens opening, and the length of time the shutter is open. The digital value produced by that energy exposure is also proportional to the ISO

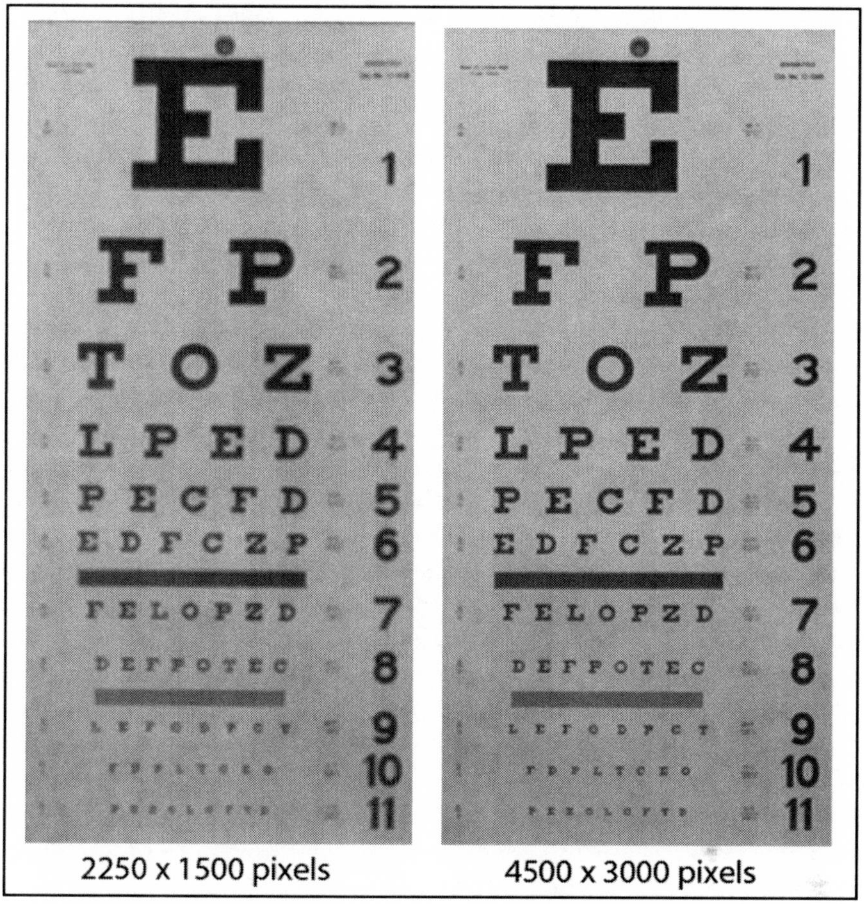

Figure 2.3 *Photograph of an eye test chart from 20 feet with two different pixel size settings.*

setting of the camera. The ISO setting is a way of controlling the amplification of the electrical signal associated with the sensor array. Increasing the ISO will increase the digital values in an image without altering the camera exposure settings. It is convenient to take all of these factors into consideration in defining the *relative exposure* as,

$$\text{Relative Exposure} = \text{ISO*T/(f-number)}^2 \qquad \text{Eq. 2.1}$$

The "f-number," abbreviated as "f/" is the ratio of the focal length of the lens to the diameter of the iris opening of the lens. It is the area of the lens opening that determines the lens contribution to exposure. The area is proportional to the square of the lens diameter, which is why the square of the f-number appears in the equation. The equation indicates that doubling the f/number (closing down the lens diameter by a factor of two) can be compensated by an increase in the shutter time by a factor of 4 to 1. This is referred to as "reciprocity." Generally as exposure time is increased, a point will be reached where this trade-off of exposure time and lens diameter will no longer exist. In the author's experience with accident investigation photography, it is not necessary to take photographs with a shutter time greater than 4 seconds. Usually, shutter times of 4 seconds or less fall within the range of reciprocity.

The three components of relative exposure offer the opportunity for various compromises with respect to the camera settings. The choice to be made depends entirely on the conditions and objective associated with the photographic task. Selection of higher ISO settings reduces shutter time which can be important in scenes in which there is motion present. Using a higher ISO setting allows use of a higher f-number. The higher f-number (reduced iris diameter) will result in increased depth of field in the image, which is the range of distances at which acceptable focus can be maintained. A higher f-number will also result in reduced halo effects. A brief description of each of these effects will follow.

To illustrate the effect of using higher ISO settings to allow shorter shutter times or higher f-number lens settings, a pair of photographs were taken of a Macbeth ColorChecker. The Macbeth ColorChecker has five rows of calibrated "patches." The top four rows are various colors and the bottom row is a series of grayscale patches. Figure 2.4 shows two photographs cropped to show only the bottom row of grayscale patches since the photo is black and white. The top photo was taken using an ISO settings of 100 and the bottom with an ISO setting of 400, with a corresponding 4 to 1 decrease in shutter time.

At first glance the two images appear to be similar. The penalty for using the higher ISO settings is that there will be more "granularity" or "noise" in the resulting image. To demonstrate the effect, Figure 2.5 shows the far right grayscale patches in both of these images and enhances them by multiplying all of the digital values by a factor of 4 to 1. This means that the digital values of 64 in these patches was increased to a digital value of 255, thus making these "noise" variations more easily visible.

For some objectives and conditions this added noise will not be important and the higher ISO setting can be used to decrease shutter time or increase depth of field with higher f-numbers; but there can be different situations where this degradation of image quality at the lower luminance levels would be undesirable.

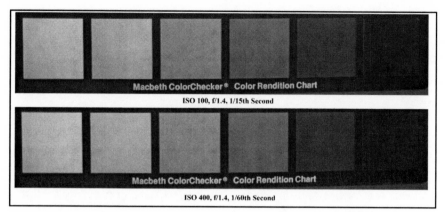

Figure 2.4 *Composite of two photographs of Macbeth grayscales with different exposure settings.*

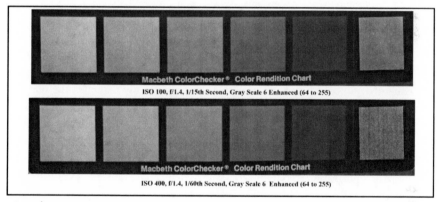

Figure 2.5 *Photographs of Figure 2.4 with darkest grayscale patch enhanced to show the granularity associated with an increase in ISO setting.*

2.8 Depth of Field

Figure 2.6 is a sketch to aid in discussing the depth of field in a photographic image. Assume that the camera lens is focused at a distance of "R focus." The lines in the sketch trace the light from the distance "R focus" to the edges of the lens and back on to the image plane at a distance (I focus) behind the lens. These lines converge to a point (within the limits of lens resolution) in the "image plane." By contrast, an object point located at a distance of "Rfar" will be imaged at a shorter distance behind the lens, "I far." As shown, the light from an object at a distance, "Rfar," will then continue on, reaching the image plane, "I focus," as a circle of light, sometimes termed the "circle of confusion." In Figure 2.6, the diameter of this circle is labelled "Blur." In other words, the image of a point of

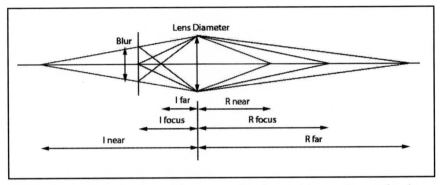

Figure 2.6 *Diagram showing the ray tracing from object to image for three different object distances.*

light at a distance "Rfar" will appear in the recorded image as a "circle of confusion" of diameter "Blur." In a similar manner, an object located at a distance of "Rnear" will be imaged at a distance from the lens of "I near," to the left of the image plane located at "I focus." The two distances, "Rfar" and "Rnear" are so chosen because they both generate a "circle of confusion" of diameter "Blur." Used herein is a slightly different definition of "depth of field" than that which is frequently quoted. The assumption that these photos are taken for the purpose of allowing a person to view them, at the proper viewing distance, and experience a realistic impression as to the level of visibility of objects in the scene. In order to accomplish that objective, it is important that the resolution of the image be equal to or greater than the resolution of the eye of the viewer. The angular resolution of an observer having 20/20 vision is 1 arc minute. Therefore, for these purposes, the depth of field is defined as that range of distances at which the photograph will have an angular resolution of 1 arc minute or better. It follows that the diameter of the "circle of confusion," that is, the "Blur," will have an angular size equal to 1 arc minute. The equations which define "Rnear" and "Rfar" are as follows:

$$\text{Rnear} = f/[1-(\text{Rfocus-f})/\text{Rfocus}+f/D*\tan(\text{phi}), \qquad \text{Eq. 2.2}$$

and,

$$\text{Rfar} = f/[1-(\text{Rfocus-f})/\text{Rfocus-f}/D*\tan(\text{phi}), \qquad \text{Eq. 2.3}$$

where "phi" is 1 arc minute, the visual resolution. Using these equations, the following numerical examples have been calculated. All distances are in feet.

Rfocus	f=50mm, f/1.4		f=50mm, f/2.8		f=50mm, f/5.6	
	Rnear	Rfar	Rnear	Rfar	Rnear	Rfar
25	24	27	22	29	20	33
50	45	57	40	67	33	99
100	80	133	67	199	50	14,330
200	134	397	100	28,661	67	Infinity
400	201	57,322	134	Infinity	80	Infinity

Rfocus	f=28mm f/1.4		f=28mm f/2.8		f=28mm f/5.6	
	Rnear	Rfar	Rnear	Rfar	Rnear	Rfar
25	13	28	13	32	11	45
50	25	64	22	90	19	441
100	45	180	37	882	28	Infinity
200	75	1,764	56	Infinity	38	Infinity
400	112	Infinity	75	Infinity	45	Infinity

2.9 Camera Calibration

RGB (red, green, blue) images commonly utilize digital values from 0 to 255 to record the magnitude of each of the three color components. A pixel that has values of R=255, G=255, B=255 is white. A pixel in which the three colors have equal value, but less than 255, is "gray." "Luminosity" is a term that simulates "luminance" by combining the red, green, and blue color values to produce a single digital value, also in the range of 0 to 255. A luminosity value is obtained by adding 30 percent of the red digital value to 59 percent of the green digital value and 11 percent of the blue digital value. Figure 2.7 shows a series of grayscale patches generated on the computer. The digital value of each patch is as shown.

As previously discussed, the quantity of light energy that reaches a pixel in the camera detector array is determined by the luminance of the corresponding element in the scene being photographed and the camera settings related to exposure. The components of exposure include the area of the lens opening in the camera, the exposure time, and the ISO setting utilized. The area of the lens is proportional to the inverse square of the f-number of the lens setting. The exposure time is the length of time the shutter is open during the exposure. The ISO is a camera setting of sensitivity, similar to the ASA ratings that were associated with film speeds. The "relative effective exposure," Q, is the product of each of these three factors, or,

$$Q = ISO*T/f^2. \hspace{2cm} \text{Eq. 2.4}$$

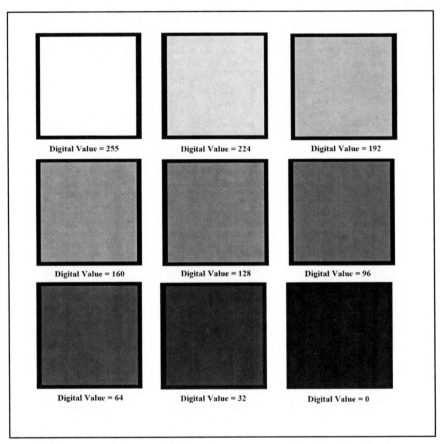

Figure 2.7 *Computer-generated nine step grayscale with digital values from 0 to 255 at intervals of 32.*

Also, as previously discussed, cameras suffer a *reciprocity failure* for long exposure times. When that exposure time is reached, it simply means that the effective exposure will be less than indicated by the actual exposure time used; so, for example, doubling the exposure time will alter the image less than doubling the lens area. For digital cameras, reciprocity failure does not typically exist for exposure times equal to or less than 4 seconds.

The product of Q and B (scene luminance or brightness) gives a numerical value proportional to the total light energy incident on each pixel in the camera sensor array. The calibration is accomplished by setting up the grayscale chart, using a spot photometer to measure the luminance of each of the grayscale patches and then photographing the chart with a wide range of exposure values (Q). In the particular calibration to be described here, 20 photographs were taken with

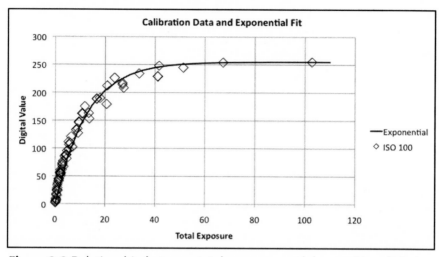

Figure 2.8 *Relationship between total exposure and the resulting digital values derived from photographs taken of the nine step grayscale.*

exposure values chosen so that the resulting pictures ranged from dramatically overexposed to dramatically underexposed. The resulting photographs are then examined on the computer to determine the digital values associated with each grayscale patch. Figure 2.8 is a graph in which the product B*Q (total exposure) is plotted against the corresponding luminosity digital value.

The graph takes on a familiar mathematical form having "exponential" characteristics. The equation used to fit the curve is:

$$DV = 255*(1\text{-}exp(\text{-}0.10*BQ)).$$
$$\text{Eq. 2.5}$$

The "exponential" data points were calculated from Equation 2.5 and provide a good fit to the measured data. When we take a photograph, we know the exposure values (Q) that were used, so we can use Equation 2.5 to determine the scene luminance, B, that corresponds to each digital value in the image. This is accomplished by solving Equation 2.5 for B, which gives,

$$B = \text{-}10.0/Q*ln(1\text{-}DV/255).$$
$$\text{Eq. 2.6}$$

The camera has now become a light meter. If we know the exposure settings, then we can use Equation 2.6 to calculate the luminance of any object in the scene. The mathematically inclined will know that "exp" stands for the exponential function, which is the value of "e" raised to the power of the value contained in the parenthesis, and that "ln" stands for the natural logarithm.

2.10 The Concept of Linearity

The fidelity of the final displayed image involves the characteristics of the camera, the nature of any computer processing that is performed on this image, and the characteristics of the display device, such as a monitor, printer, or projector. Each of these devices will be discussed in the sections that follow. Before doing so it is of importance to discuss the significance of "linearity." In the digital world, the image detail associated with each pixel is defined in terms of digital values between 0 and 255 for each of three different colors: red, green, and blue, and the manner in which this numerical detail is processed by the camera and the involved display devices: monitors, printers, and projectors. If we have two elements of detail in the scene, one of which is twice as bright as the other, then we need to insure that this is also true in terms of the final displayed image. If we use a light meter to measure the luminance of a series of objects in the scene and then make the same measurements in the final displayed image, we can test the linearity of the process. If we graph the "scene" luminance versus the "screen" luminance, the graph will be a straight line if linearity is present. If linearity is not present then the contrast of objects will not be realistically presented. For colored objects, the absence of linearity will also result in color distortion, since each of the red, green and blue components will be subject to different treatment. The final objective of obtaining photographs that realistically convey visibility is to correct the overall process to produce a final product in which linearity is achieved.

2.11 Image Linearity

To achieve true image fidelity, the digital value of the recorded image should be directly proportional to the scene luminance. For such a "linear" image, doubling the scene luminance would double the digital value. The exponential fit curve illustrates a mathematical fit to the camera non-linearity, which, for the mathematically inclined, can be a useful tool.

The direction of the departure from linearity in the camera means that objects in the scene with larger digital values will be shown at reduced contrast and will therefore be more difficult to see. For family photos, this is not a significant problem. For forensic photography dealing with visibility issues, it is necessary to consider this non-linearity in terms of the objectives of the photograph. If the purpose in showing the pictures is to demonstrate that objects in the scene are clearly visible, and if these objects in the photo are indeed clearly visible in spite of the decrease in contrast generated by the nonlinearity, then there is no problem. If the non-linearity did not exist, the objects in the scene would be even more visible than depicted by the photo. If, on the other hand, the objective is to demonstrate that objects are difficult to see, then the contrast reduction due to the

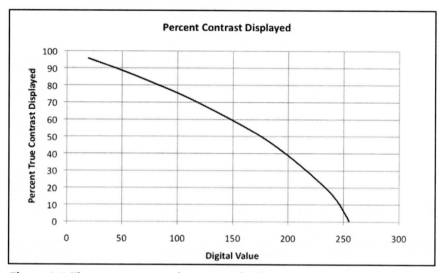

Figure 2.9 *The percentage reduction in displayed contrast due to camera non-linearity.*

non-linearity in the pictures may raise serious questions as to the legitimacy of the photographs.

Figure 2.9 shows the reduction in contrast resulting from the camera non-linearity. The curve shows that for a low contrast object having a background with a digital value of 50, the displayed contrast will be a little less than 90 percent of its true value. However, if the digital value of the background is 150, the displayed contrast will be reduced to approximately 60 percent of its true value. As indicated in the previous paragraph, it is necessary to consider the specific visibility issues associated with the use of these photographs in order to make an accurate assessment as to whether the non-linearity damages the credibility of the presentation.

2.12 Correction for Non-Linearity

If the non-linearity presents a problem, then there is an easy solution. Photo processing software, such as Photoshop, makes it possible to modify an image by inserting a "curve" that takes each digital value and replaces it with a corrected digital value. For the sample data that has been shown here, Figure 2.10 shows the correction curve, "Linear," that would need to be applied. As you can see, with such a correction, all digital values greater than approximately 160 will have a digital value of 255, that is, "saturated." If in fact there is detail of interest in this 160 to 255 digital value region, then an alternative way of achieving linearity can be used. For example in Figure 2.10, the curve, "Linearity Div 2," offers a correction which is the equivalent of having reduced the exposure used

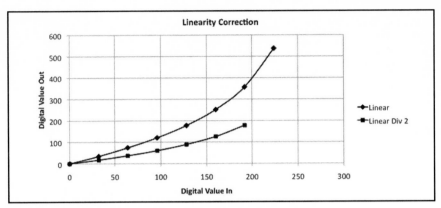

Figure 2.10 *Correction factors for camera non-linearity.*

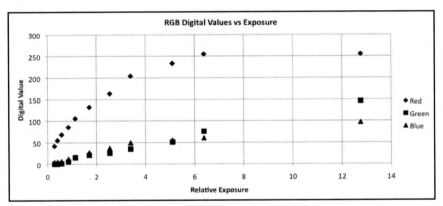

Figure 2.11 *Illustrating the nature of the color distortion in a photograph due to camera non-linearity.*

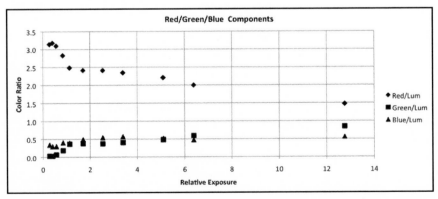

Figure 2.12 *Nature of the color distortion due to camera non-linearity as a function of the ratio of each color component (RGB) to the luminosity.*

for the photograph by a factor of 2 so that detail in the 160 to 255 digital value region is retained. The factor of 2 is just an example. Any numerical factor for exposure reduction can be used in the process.

There is one additional benefit to making the non-linearity correction. In the digital world, the color of an object is determined by the relative magnitude of the red, green and blue digital values. With a gray object there will be equal values of red, green and blue (RGB). For a gray object, each of these components will suffer the same loss in value due to the non-linearity. A colored object, however, will not have equal values and whichever RGB component is higher will, in the presence of non-linearity, be reduced in value by a greater amount than the reduction for the other color components, thereby altering the relative magnitude of the RGB values and distorting the color. Because of the nonlinearity, the higher the digital value of the principal color, the more the color will be distorted. With increased exposure, all colors will be driven towards "white." For example, in a nighttime scene where the target of interest is of low brightness value, a red traffic light may become totally saturated and will therefore be recorded as a digital value of 255 for all three colors, that is, "white." Figure 2.11 is a graph that shows the measurements of the digital values of the RGB components of the "red" patch on the Macbeth ColorChecker from photos taken over a wide range of exposure settings. The sensation of color comes from the ratio of each of the three color components to the "luminosity." Those ratios are shown in Figure 2.12. As the graph shows, each of these three ratios is headed toward a value of unity as the exposure is increased, in other words, headed towards "white."

Obtaining an image in which the luminance and color are accurately represented by the digital values is only the start of the process. The images are viewed as printer output, on our monitors, or from projection equipment. Therefore it is necessary to look at the characteristics of our printers, monitors, and projectors.

2.13 Printer Output

There are obviously many different computer printers on the market and there is no attempt made herein to investigate the variations in performance that they represent. The author's current printer is a combination print, fax, scan, and copy machine. It produces "nice looking" output. The computer-generated grayscale shown in Figure 2.7 was printed on both plain and glossy (photo) paper. A spot photometer was then used to measure the luminance of each of the nine patches. The glossy paper was positioned such that there would be no mirror-like reflections from the glossy surface. The luminance measurements were normalized such that the maximum value (white) had a value of 255. Figure 2.13 is a graph showing the results. Included in the graph is a straight line (linear) which shows what would exist if the printed image had luminance values directly proportional

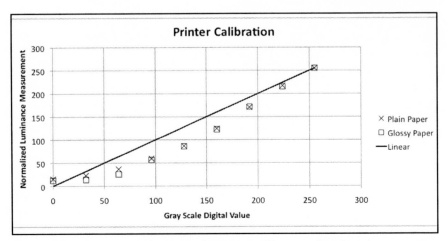

Figure 2.13 *Printer non-linearity documented by printing the nine step gray.*

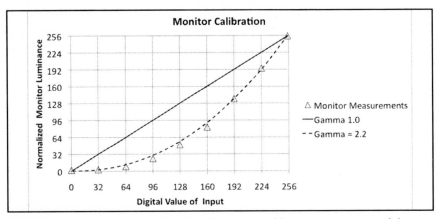

Figure 2.14 *Monitor non-linearity documented by measurement of the luminance of the displayed nine step grayscale.*

to input digital values, which is the requirement for fidelity. The graph shows that the printouts for both papers are pretty close to linearity, with a "gamma" a little greater than 1.0.

What is also apparent in the graph is that the luminance of the printout bottoms out as it reaches the lower digital value region. For the patch with the digital value of 0 (black) the plain paper has a digital value of 15 and the glossy paper 12. This means that the total range of luminance values that can be displayed is 17 to 1 for the plain paper and 21 to 1 for the glossy paper. This is the result of the fact that "total black" from the printer has a reflectance of about 6 percent for the plain paper and 5 percent for the glossy paper.

2.14 Monitor Calibration

The term "gamma" is frequently used with respect to the characteristics of display devices. The definition of gamma is that the display luminance of each pixel in a scene is proportional to the digital value raised to the gamma power. For example, with a gamma equal to 2.0, a two to one range of digital values will result in a four to one range (two squared) of displayed luminance. This results in very pleasant, high contrast images. Photographic film users want to see high contrast in their end products. Some computer monitors can calibrate the display to alter the gamma of the presentation. The recommendation that comes along with these instructions is that the built-in gamma of 2.2 be used. The nine-step grayscale patches previously described were displayed on a calibrated monitor. The room was darkened to eliminate the effect of any room light, and a spot photometer was used to measure the luminance of each of the nine patches. The set of readings were normalized such that the highest luminance value measured became 255. Figure 2.14 is a graph showing the measurements with the actual monitor luminance measurements shown as the dashed line. The graph includes calculated values for a gamma of 2.2 and a gamma of 1.0, meaning that the luminance of the displayed image would be directly proportional to the digital value being displayed. The actual monitor luminance measurements are a good match to the "recommended gamma" of 2.2.

The gamma 2.2 setting produces "nice looking pictures." However, if the objective is to show someone the true appearance of a scene, these monitor images do not properly show the contrasts of objects in that scene and may cause false judgments to be made with respect to visibility issues. To illustrate that point, Figure 2.15 shows distortion of contrast which results from a gamma 2.2 display of the images.

Figure 2.15 shows the displayed contrast as a function of the actual contrast. The "Gamma 1.0 Display" line emphasizes what should be displayed if the objective is to realistically show the contrast that exists in a scene. The numerical values associated with the graph are as follows:

Actual Contrast	Displayed Contrast
-1.00	-1.00
-0.75	-0.95
-0.50	-0.78
-0.25	-0.47
0.00	0.00
0.25	0.63
0.50	1.44
0.75	2.43
1.00	3.59

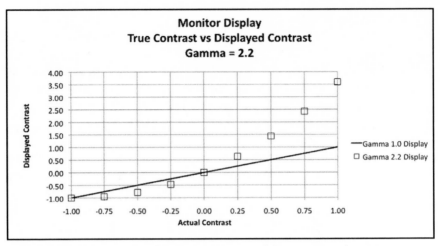

Figure 2.15 *Monitor non-linearity in terms of the contrast distortion.*

Only two values of actual contrast are properly displayed: -1.00 and 0.00. The contrast of -1.00 means that the target object is totally black, and the contrast of 0.00 (target object is a perfect match to the luminance of the background and is therefore not visible). For a positive contrast of 1.00 (target object twice the luminance of the background), the displayed contrast is 3.59 times the actual contrast. If the objective is to allow a viewer to form a judgment as to what can and cannot be seen, this is an unacceptable distortion.

The monitor luminance measurements showed a range of approximately 250 to 1, which is considerably better than the 21 to 1 measured for the printer output on glossy paper.

2.15 Projector Calibration

The author has used three different projectors for courtroom presentation of nighttime scene photographs. Each had quite different display characteristics. The one currently being used offers settings for both "brightness" and "contrast" ranging from -50 to +50. The results produced by alterations of either of these two control settings are not in agreement with the technical definitions of "brightness" and "contrast." For example, a true "brightness" control would not produce any modifications of "contrast," which is not the case for this particular projector. It was necessary to explore the results of various combinations of these two settings to see what effect it had on the brightness and contrast of the displayed image. The current projector being used has a high "gamma." That is, the screen luminance increases more than linearly with increase in digital value. The camera has non-linearity in the opposite direction, that is, an increase in

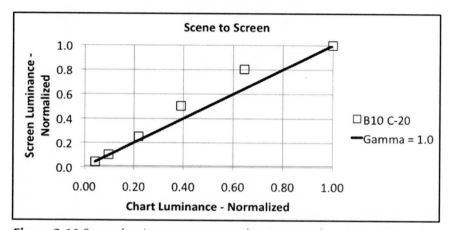

Figure 2.16 *Scene luminance vs. screen luminance of a projected scene photograph.*

scene luminance produces less than a linear increase in digital value. This means that the projector acts in the direction of correcting for the non-linearity of the camera. It is certainly not an accurate correction. This does suggest, however, that rather than making independent corrections of the camera and the projector, there is merit to considering a "scene to screen" correction where a single correction process causes the projected screen luminance to be a linear match to the actual scene luminance.

A "scene to screen" correction can be accomplished in a three-step process. Step 1 is to use the spot photometer to measure the luminance values of each of the six Macbeth ColorChecker grayscale patches. Step 2 is to photograph the Macbeth ColorChecker. Step 3 is to project that unmodified digital image and measure the luminance of each of the six grayscale patches in the projected image. Figure 2.16 is a graph showing chart luminance (normalized) plotted against screen luminance (normalized). The normalization process consists of dividing each of the six chart luminance measurements by the luminance of the brightest grayscale patch and dividing each of the six screen luminance measurements by the luminance of the projection of the brightest grayscale patch.

For the graph, the projector settings (B10 C-20) are selected to come reasonably close to achieving linearity (gamma = 1.0). If a projector does not have settings that result in reasonable proximity to linearity, then a Photoshop correction needs to be calculated and applied to the images to be projected similar to those illustrated in Figure 2.15.

2.16 Adjusting the Luminance of the Projected Image

As previously stated, one of the factors that determines visual performance is the luminance level of the scene. If a photograph is viewed at luminance levels much higher than those that existed at the scene, the level of detail visible to the observer will be greater than that which would have been visible at the scene even though the angular size and contrast levels have been properly reproduced. For scene detail of low contrast and angular size, incorrect luminance levels can result in invalid opinions as to visibility. If this is the case, it becomes important to display the photos at the true brightness levels.[1] For example, at a scene luminance of 0.1 foot-Lamberts but displayed at 10 foot-Lamberts, the contrast levels required to allow visual detection will have to be reduced by a factor of about 3.69 to 1.[2] If the object detail of interest in the picture is of high enough contrast such that a reduction in contrast by this amount will not alter the viewer's opinions with respect to visibility, then the requirement to reduce the brightness of the projected scene is not a critical issue.

A direct way of accomplishing the reduction of the brightness of the projected image is to darken the courtroom and use neutral density filters to reduce the output of the projector. We have experienced a number of situations where this could not be accomplished. Some courtrooms have windows allowing direct daylight illumination. This was the situation the very first time we used this technique in court. In that case the projection of the images was moved to the windowless jury room where total darkening could be accomplished. In another trial, the judge declined to darken the courtroom for security reasons.

The procedure which we have used for using neutral density filters to reduce the projected luminance involves generating a digital image consisting of a grayscale patch, having a digital value of 100, located on a black background. Using Equation 2.2, knowing the camera exposure settings used to generate the photos that we want to project, we can calculate the luminance that this patch should have in order to reproduce the scene lighting. We project this patch image and measure it with a spot photometer in the courtroom to determine the reduction in brightness that must be made. Neutral density filters are commercially available. They are called "neutral" because they reduce all colors by the same amount. The filters are labelled in terms of the logarithm to the base 10 of the reciprocal of the transmission of the filter. For example, a filter generating a 2 to 1 reduction in transmitted light (transmittance of 0.5) is labeled as 0.3 which is the logarithm to the base 10 of 2.0. A filter generating a 4 to 1 reduction in transmitted light is labeled 0.6, and a filter with a 10 to 1 reduction is labeled 1.0, and so on.

A question that arises is, "just how dark does the courtroom need to be?" Contrast is defined by the equation,

$$C = (B_T - B_B)/B_B. \qquad\qquad \text{Eq. 2.7}$$

Where B_T is the luminance of the target of interest and B_B is the luminance of the background against which the target is viewed. If there is stray light falling on the screen, coming from sources other than the projector, then the contrast of objects in the scene will be reduced. The equation that describes this reduction is,

$$C_S = ((B_T + B_S) - (B_B + B_S))/(B_B + B_S), \qquad\qquad \text{Eq. 2.8}$$

Where C_S is the contrast in the presence of the stray light and B_S is the luminance of the stray light in the room, which is added to both the target and background. Equation 2.4 reduces to,

$$C_S = (B_T - B_B)/((B_B + B_S)). \qquad\qquad \text{Eq. 2.9}$$

The percentage reduction in contrast is,

$$100*C_S/C = 100* B_B/ (B_B + B_S). \qquad\qquad \text{Eq. 2.10}$$

As an example, if the luminance of the stray room light on the projection screen had a value equal to the luminance of the background against which the target of interest is being viewed, the contrast would be reduced to 50 percent of its true value.

There is another alternative which is useful under certain circumstances. Suppose that you need to reduce the luminance of the projected image by a factor of 10 to 1 to achieve scene luminance. That would mean using a 1.0 neutral density filter. Instead of using a neutral density filter to achieve the 10 to 1 reduction, we can project the image onto a "black" screen having a reflectance of 10 percent. This not only generates the needed 10 to 1 reduction in the luminance of the projected image but also reduces the stray light in the room by a factor of 10 to 1, thereby dramatically reducing the contrast reduction associated with the stray light.

2.17 Miscellaneous Photographic Techniques

Sometimes it happens that the lighting at the scene has changed since the time of the accident. For example, assume the accident involved a collision in which an automobile struck the rear of a stationary automobile. Assume that it was determined that a streetlight had been added since the accident. This would raise the question as to whether photographs taken at a site inspection, using exemplar vehicles, would distort the visibility issues involved as far as the moving vehicle driver's capability of sighting the stationary vehicle by virtue of the lighting associated with only the two vehicles. One approach to solving this problem is to take a pair of photographs at each of the set of measured distances prior to impact. One of these photographs would involve all of the present lighting of the scene including the lighting associated with both vehicles and the newly installed streetlight. The second photograph would be taken after turning off all lighting generated by the two vehicles. Using software, like Photoshop, the second photograph can be subtracted from the first photograph, removing all lighting from the streetlight. Prior to performing the subtraction process, both photographs need to be corrected to remove nonlinearity.

2.18 Camera Use as a Light Meter in Scenes with High Range of Luminance Values

As previously mentioned, night scenes with artificial illumination can result in scene luminance values that far exceed the range that can be captured with the digital camera. When exposure settings are used that reasonably capture the scene detail of interest, high luminance objects such as light sources will appear in the image with total saturation so that the red, blue, and green digital values will all take on a value of 255. This means that neither the color nor the luminance of these light sources can be determined from the photographs. From a visibility viewpoint, there can be times when it is important to have knowledge of the actual color and luminance of these light sources relative to other objects in the scene. This can be accomplished by taking a series of photos with a large enough range of exposure settings such that, after linear correction, the images of the light sources in the scene are recorded without saturation. These images can be used to calculate the actual luminance values and to allow visualization of their true color.

2.19 Distance Estimates From Photographs

On accident site visits it is common to take a series of photos at selected distances from an accident impact area. Ordinarily, this is accomplished by marking off the desired distances, positioning the camera at each location and shooting the pictures. However, on occasion photos need to be taken at times that match the lighting conditions of the accident despite traffic conditions that disfavor this procedure. The investigator might have to repeatedly drive the route and shoot pictures during brief gaps in traffic. This results in photos at distances that had not been previously measured and marked. This is an example of a situation in which photometric techniques can be of value. To illustrate this technique, picture that the camera is aimed directly ahead down the roadway. Also assume that there is some object, like a roadway sign, located along the right side of the street and that the sign is oriented so that the flat surface of the sign is perpendicular to the roadway. The dimensions of the sign can be measured at a convenient time, before or after the photography is accomplished. Given the focal length of the lens, the dimensions of the camera image detector array, and the horizontal pixel count of the recorded imagery, the angular size of the sign can be calculated from each photograph. Knowing the dimensions of the sign allows its angular size to be translated into the distance of the sign. Finally, knowing the position of the sign relative to a suitable scene reference point allows direct determination of the camera position relative to this reference point.

A convenient first step in making photometric calculations is to determine the "pixel equivalent" of the focal length of the lens. Let us assume a camera has a maximum setting of 4500 horizontal pixels, covering the 36mm sensor array. Using a 50mm focal length lens, the pixel equivalent of the focal length is 4500*50/36 or 6,250 pixels. As an illustrative example, assume that the left side of a sign is located 1000 pixels from the center of the image and that the right side of the sign is located 1200 pixels from the center of the image. The equations involved in calculating the distance to the sign are as follows.

Let X be the physical distance of the left side of the sign from the centerline of the camera pointed down the road, and R is the distance from the camera to the extension of the sign directly to the left, intersecting the centerline of the camera aim. Theta Left is the angular position of the left side of the sign and Theta Right is the angular position of the right side of the sign. Then,

$$X/R = \tan (\text{Theta Left}), \qquad \text{Eq. 2.11}$$

and,

$$(X+W)/R = \tan (\text{Theta Right}). \qquad \text{Eq. 2.12}$$

Subtracting Equation 2.11 from Equation 2.12 results in,

$$W/R = \tan (\text{Theta Right}) - \tan (\text{Theta Left}). \qquad \text{Eq. 2.13}$$

So that,

$$R = W/[\tan (\text{Theta Right}) - \tan (\text{Theta Left})] \qquad \text{Eq. 2.14}$$

If the width of the sign, W, is 3 feet then,

$$R = 3/(1200/6250 - 1000/6250) = 93.75 \text{ feet} \qquad \text{Eq. 2.15}$$

2.20 Summary

Visual capability for achieving detection, recognition, and identification are dramatically dependent upon the scene light levels, the contrast of the object of interest, the angular size of that object, and the time available to accomplish the task. This chapter described techniques for generating courtroom display of imagery such that the light levels, contrast, and angular size are reproduced with reasonable accuracy. This involved the calibration of the equipment involved such as the camera, monitor, printer, and projector. The specific calibrations presented were performed on the author's own equipment. The author has calibrated three different cameras, each of which produced very similar results. The total luminance range of printer images is limited to the relative reflectance of the white paper as compared with the reflectance of that paper fully covered with a layer of black ink. For that reason, any printer will likely produce results similar to what is noted in this chapter. With respect to your monitor and projector, there are generally settings involved and there are substantial differences among equipment. For that reason, to obtain a scene accurate presentation it would be necessary for you to perform a calibration similar to that which is described.

There are two other important factors involved in a courtroom presentation of scene photos. The first has to do with the timing associated with the presentation. In many accidents, the important events take place in a relatively short period of time. Site visits are made under lighting conditions similar to that which would have existed at the time of the accident with the reconstructionist marking off locations of the parties involved at specific times prior to impact, such as for example, 1-second intervals. Photos taken from an exemplar vehicle at these locations depicting these time intervals can then be used to generate a PowerPoint presentation duplicating the view at these specific times. Viewing such a time-sequence duplication may produce quite different, and more realistic, impressions than would be produced with an unlimited observation time of the images. The second factor has to do with recognizing the importance of the mental priority list of the parties involved which would determine their visual search, that is, where they were pointing their eyes. If everyone in the courtroom is aware that the accident involved a pedestrian approaching from the driver's left, then when shown a photograph of the driver's view, they will be looking to the left, whereas the driver, having no knowledge of the impending encounter, may well have been looking straight ahead, or to the right. In an effort to compensate for this effect, it can be important to display the sequence a number of times with the jury requested to view the sequence while fixating in a specific direction, as for example, straight ahead, or to the right side of the roadway, and so on, while viewing the photos.

Even with all of this care, it is difficult to make the viewing experience a completely accurate representation of how it would have appeared to the party involved in the accident. However, it may generate far more accurate impressions of the visibility issues than those created by verbal testimony from experts on the two sides, insisting that the party "should have been able to" or "would not have been able to" accomplish the visual task associated with accident avoidance.

Endnotes

1. Harris, James L. Sr., and James L. Harris II, "Forensic Photography and Nighttime Visibility Issues," *Journal of Forensic Sciences*, July 1992.

2. Blackwell, H. R.: "Contrast Thresholds of the Human Eye," *J. Opt. Soc. Amer.*, 36, 11, 24-643 (1946).

Chapter 3

Pedestrian and Automobile Accidents

3.1 Pedestrian/Vehicle Accidents

Every accident deserves to be analyzed on its own without generalization as to where the fault lies. However, one generalization that can be made is that, when there is a collision between a vehicle and a pedestrian, the pedestrian will suffer the serious and often fatal injuries that result. With this in mind, it is certainly in the best interest of pedestrians to play a major defensive role, doing everything in their power to avoid an accident even under conditions in which they feel that they clearly have the right of way. Pedestrians should never assume that vehicle drivers will see them and take necessary avoidance actions, and they should never cross the path of an oncoming vehicle unless they have clear visual evidence that the driver is taking action to slow or stop the vehicle so as to prevent an accident.

One daytime pedestrian-vehicle accident that the author encountered involved a pedestrian crossing the street in a marked crosswalk, with two lanes in each direction of travel. A vehicle in the right lane had stopped at the crosswalk to allow the pedestrian to cross. A second vehicle, approaching the crosswalk in the left lane, did not see the pedestrian because the vehicle in the right lane blocked the line of sight. Of course it is reasonable to consider that the driver of the second vehicle should have recognized that the presence of a stopped vehicle in the right lane might indicate there was a pedestrian crossing. In this particular accident, the pedestrian stepped forward into the left lane just as the vehicle in that lane entered the crosswalk. Independent of the arguments as to the right of way and causation, the pedestrian could have avoided this collision by pausing and looking to the left to make sure there was no oncoming traffic before entering the left lane.

The vast majority of pedestrian-vehicle accidents the author has encountered have taken place at night, where the important variables include the headlight and streetlight illumination, pedestrian clothing reflectance, and the nature of the background against which the pedestrian is viewed. This discussion will therefore be directed toward nighttime accidents.

3.2 The Collision Triangle

Accidents generally involve the collision of two objects each traveling along paths that intersect at the point of impact. In many cases, the velocity of each object is nearly constant for some period of time prior to impact. These conditions are geometrically described in terms of a *collision triangle*.

Figure 3.1 shows two objects approaching a point of collision, in this example, at right angles to each other. Drawing lines connecting the location of each party and the point of impact generates a collision triangle. The length of the side labeled "V1*t" is proportional to the product of the velocity of "Object 1" multiplied by "t," the time to impact. The length of the side labeled "V2*t" is proportional to the velocity of "Object 2" multiplied by "t," the time to impact. "R" is the distance between the two objects. "A" is the bearing angle, measured from the direction of travel of Object 1, at which an observer at that location has to look in order to see Object 2. In a similar fashion, "B" is the angle measured from the direction of travel of Object 2 at which an observer in that location has to look to see Object 1. If the velocity of the two objects does not change throughout the encounter, then as the distance to the point of impact decreases, the triangle becomes smaller but the shape of the triangle does not change. This means that the bearing angles A and B will remain the same. This is termed "constancy of bearing." It is the criterion historically used to determine the threat of collision by ships and aircraft. If the "target" does not change its angular position with time, it poses a possible collision threat. It is important to recognize that under conditions of "constant bearing" the peripheral vision attribute of detection of motion plays a limited role. In most cases it would be expected that the speed of the vehicle will be significantly greater than the speed of the pedestrian. As previously stated, "constancy of bearing" exists for situations in which the two parties to a collision maintain constant velocity throughout the encounter. This statement would only be precisely true if the eye of the vehicle driver collides with the pedestrian at impact. To illustrate this point, assume that the pedestrian is coming from the driver's left side and ends up colliding near the right front of the vehicle. For the purpose of illustration, assume that this point of impact is 5 feet forward and 2 feet to the right of the driver's eye position. Further assume that the vehicle is traveling at 30 miles per hour and the pedestrian at 4 feet per second. Figure 3.2 shows the bearing angle of the pedestrian as viewed by the driver for the last 10 seconds until impact.

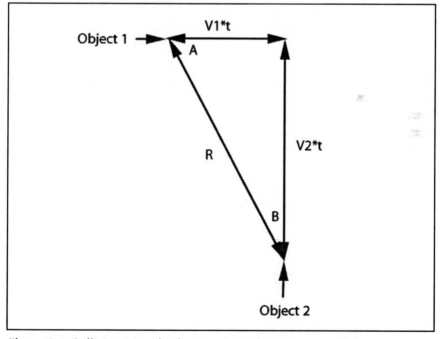

Figure 3.1 Collision triangle showing two objects on a collision course and the bearing angles associated with such an encounter.

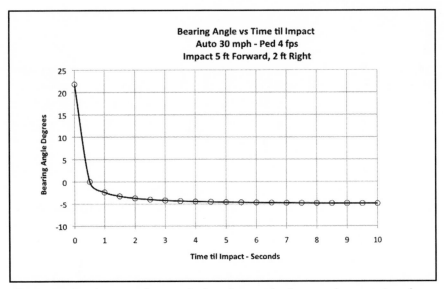

Figure 3.2 *Pre-impact changes in bearing angle that can be associated with a collision.*

As Figure 3.2 indicates, for the time period from 10 to 2 seconds before impact, the bearing angle is about -5 degrees, meaning 5 degrees to the driver's left, and then during the last two seconds before impact, moves rapidly to the driver's right. The collision takes place at a bearing angle of a little over 20 degrees to the driver's right. Under these circumstances, it would not be surprising to read a driver's statement that, just a few seconds before impact, the pedestrian was seen moving rapidly from the left to the right. Note that 2 seconds is slightly greater than the frequently quoted perception-reaction time, so that if the driver's first sighting is at 2 seconds before impact, the collision is almost certain to happen.

There are a number of factors related to constancy of bearing. First of all, when an object is viewed in the periphery, motion can be an important aid to visual acquisition. The periphery has some sensitivity to motion, calling our attention to objects, which then leads to eye movements to bring the object into the central fovea, where it can be detected and recognized. With constancy of bearing, the main body of the pedestrian continues to appear at the same position in the driver's field of view and the peripheral sensitivity to motion is not a significant factor. The term "main body" of the pedestrian is used because, in the process of restaging nighttime vehicle pedestrian accidents, the author has encountered, on a number of occasions, situations in which the dominant visual cue as to the presence of the pedestrian was the movement of a pair of white tennis shoes worn by the pedestrian. On the other hand, the author has also been involved in the investigation of an accident involving a pedestrian on a skate-board, where, in a coast phase, the arm and leg movements were not present, and, therefore, motion did not aid in achieving peripheral visual detection.

Window post obstruction of the field of view is always a consideration in vehicle encounters and becomes more significant if there is constancy of bearing. The bearing angle of this obstruction is dependent on the geometry of the particular vehicle and the seat position of the driver. As an example, for a vehicle and seat position, let us assume the bearing angle of the left window post is approximately 20 degrees to the left. Two constant velocity objects on collision course would have to have a speed ratio of about three to one to appear at that bearing angle (e.g., 4 miles per hour for the pedestrian and 12 miles per hour for the vehicle). In the vehicle/pedestrian accidents the author has encountered, the speed ratio has been considerably higher than three to one and window post obstruction of the line of sight has not been an issue.

3.3 Driver Sighting of a Pedestrian Making a Mid-Block Crossing

Headlights play a dominant role when a pedestrian makes a mid-block crossing with no crosswalk and no street lighting. These are particularly difficult situations for the driver because there will generally be no reason for the driver to be expecting such a mid-block crossing. For this reason the driver's fixation is likely to be directed forward. The other factor is that perception-reaction times can be expected to somewhat increase for unexpected events. Low beam headlights are aimed down and to the right so as to minimize glare for oncoming drivers. To illustrate the significance of the low beam headlight illumination, consider the following example. Assume a vehicle is travelling 40 miles per hour (58.7 feet per second). A commonly used perception-reaction time is 1.5 seconds. During that time period the vehicle would travel 88 feet. If the driver then applied full locked wheel braking, it would take approximately 2.6 seconds for the vehicle to come to a stop, during which time the vehicle would travel an additional 76 feet. The total distance traveled from the initiation of perception-reaction to a full stop would therefore involve 164 feet of travel taking a total of 4.1 seconds. During that 4.1-second time interval the pedestrian at 4 feet per second would have traveled 16.4 feet. Depending on the accident geography, the pedestrian might not even have been in the street 4.1 seconds before impact. Figure 3.3 shows the headlight illumination of the pedestrian as a function of horizontal bearing angle at heights above ground level of 0.14 feet, 3.00 feet, and 5.86 feet provided by a single low beam headlight at distances of 164 feet. The calculations assumed a headlight height of 3.0 feet above ground level.

Forensic Visibility

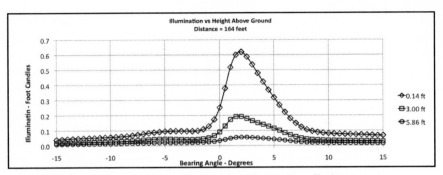

Figure 3.3 *Illumination provided by a low beam headlight at various heights above ground level at a distance of 164 feet as a function of the bearing angle.*

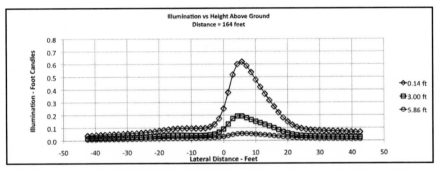

Figure 3.4 *Headlight illumination data of Figure 3.3 as a function of the lateral distance of the target.*

Figure 3.4 is a similar graph where the horizontal axis is the lateral distance associated with the bearing angle.

Published data suggest that the walking speed of pedestrians ranges from 2.5 to 6.0 feet per second with an average of approximately 4.0 feet per second.[1] Using the collision triangle, with a 40 mph vehicle and a 4 foot per second pedestrian, the horizontal bearing angle would be approximately 4 degrees. The low-beam headlight illumination in foot candles 4 degrees to the right or left at a distance of 164 feet is as follows:

Height Above Ground (Feet)	Distance (Feet)	Headlight Illum- fc	
		Ped To Right	Ped to Left
0.14	164	0.427	0.098
3.00	164	0.14	0.043
5.86	164	0.05	0.019

Figure 3.5a *(top) Image generated with computer animation software to show a roadway with a cylinder located at 164 feet as it would appear illuminated with a light source with uniform intensity in all directions.* **Figure 3.5b** *(bottom) The same as Figure 3.5a but with the light source modified to have the directional intensity associated with a typical low beam headlight.*

Civil twilight is "the limit at which twilight illumination is generally considered sufficient, under good weather conditions, for terrestrial objects to be clearly distinguished."[2] The natural illumination at civil twilight is approximately 0.3 foot-candle. Such a definition should not be considered as an accurate assessment of visibility, but is a convenient aid in visualizing the significance of scene light levels. Using this civil twilight illumination as a reference point, you can see that, at 164 feet, all of the headlight illumination values at the selected heights above ground level for pedestrians coming from the left are well below the 0.3 foot-candle level. For example the illumination of the pedestrian 3.0 feet above ground level is 0.043, approximately 7 to 1 below the twilight level; and 5.86 feet above ground level the illumination is nearly 16 to 1 below the twilight level. As expected, the headlight illumination is substantially less for a pedestrian coming from the driver's left compared to the right. But even from the right, the illumination of the pedestrian only exceeds the 0.3 foot-candle level at 0.14 feet above ground level.

Pictorial representations can often be more effective than numerical evaluation in evaluating visibility issues. With that in mind, animation software is used to generate a simplified section of roadway with a white curb on each side. A "pedestrian" cylinder is created consisting of six separate stacked cylinders each

1-foot high and 1.5 feet in diameter. The bottom cylinder has a reflectance of 85 percent, duplicating "white" clothing that has been measured. The next higher cylinder has a reflectance of 10, duplicating black pants that have been measured. The remaining four cylinders alternate between "white" and "black" up to the top cylinder (5 to 6 feet), which is "black." Using the same numerical values previously assumed (vehicle 40 miles per hour, pedestrian 4 feet per second, perception-reaction time 1.5 seconds) the total vehicle distance travelled from the initiation of perception-reaction to a locked wheel braking to a stop of 164 feet, and a pedestrian travel of 16.4 feet, these assumptions are integrated into the street scene to demonstrate the visibility of the pedestrian at the time that the driver would have to initiate the perception-reaction process in order to come to a complete stop at the 164 foot pedestrian distance. This was a two-step process. The first step, shown in Figure 3.5a, is a view of this scene illuminated by a light source having equal intensity in all directions. The illumination falls off as the square of the distance to objects in the scene, as is the case for all light sources.

The second step, shown in Figure 3.5b is to modify the light source to put in the directional properties of a low beam headlight.

Even the "white" portions of the "pedestrian" are somewhat difficult to see to the left, even more so with increase in the height above ground level. The "black" portions of the "pedestrian" viewed against a dark background would be virtually invisible. Hopefully this example illustrates the danger imposed by dark clothing. Of course there may be situations in which there is a bright background, and the pedestrian in dark clothing may be visible as a negative contrast. In forming opinions about visibility from Figure 3.5b it is important to take into consideration that, viewing this picture, we are most probably seeing the image at light levels well above the levels that would exist at the scene. For example luminance measurements were made of a print of Figure 3.5b as viewed in an office setting and these showed that the scene detail is roughly 50 times the actual luminance that would exist at the scene. This means low-level contrasts are much easier to see in an office than they would be at the scene. If, about one-half hour after sunset, you took the print outdoors to a location with no artificial illumination, you would get a more reliable impression of the true visibility of the "pedestrian." The image covers a field of view of 30 degrees. To view the image with the proper angular size, the viewing distance should be approximately twice the width of the image.

It is somewhat ironic that, with this accident geometry, a pedestrian crossing the street from the driver's right could present an even more difficult situation in that the pedestrian may not even enter the street until after the time to impact is less than the time required for the driver to complete the perception-reaction and braking required to avoid the collision.

3.4 Photographic Documentation

Listed herein are some important variables involved in attempting to determine the driver's capability for visually sighting a pedestrian performing a mid-block crossing. It is a lengthy list and the conclusions will depend upon the specific details of the situation for any given accident. It is unlikely that a verbal description of the accident conditions will provide a juror with a convincing basis for a decision as to the driver's responsibility. A more effective approach is to go to the scene under similar lighting conditions, use an exemplar pedestrian, appropriately dressed, and an exemplar vehicle with comparable headlights, and take a series of photographs at a sequence of pedestrian and vehicle positions prior to impact. Such photographs presented in a time sequence consistent with the actual accident conditions can be very convincing evidence to a jury. Photographs can also be very misleading evidence if not taken and presented properly as discussed in Chapter 2. Even with these procedures in place, there is still one remaining factor that requires attention. By the time these photos are shown in the courtroom, the jury is most likely aware of the details of the accident, for example, that this is an accident in which a pedestrian crossed the street from the driver's left. Given that information, when jurors looks at a photograph, it can be expected that they will concentrate on looking to the driver's left to see the pedestrian and, with that advantage, draw a different conclusion about driver responsibility. With that in mind, it is important to perform a courtroom experiment in which the jurors are asked to fixate on a particular location, as for example, straight down the street, or to the right side of the street to see how this alters their perception of the driver's capability to see the pedestrian. Even that leaves the juror's with one advantage that did not exist for the driver: even though they are fixating straight ahead or to the right side of the street, their mental concentration may still be on the peripheral region in which they know the pedestrian is going to appear. These are the same kinds of bias that an accident investigator also faces when he views the exemplar pedestrian at the accident scene, knowing full well where the pedestrian will appear.

3.5 Pedestrian Sighting of an Oncoming Vehicle While Making a Mid-Block Crossing

Much more time is spent discussing a driver's ability to see a pedestrian than the pedestrian's ability to see an oncoming vehicle. This is likely in part because the driver's capabilities and limitations for seeing the pedestrian are considerably more complex than the pedestrian's capabilities and limitation for seeing the oncoming vehicle. The net result is that there is a concentration on discussing the driver's role as compared with the pedestrian's role. This may end up placing a bias on the relative importance of the actions of the two parties involved in the accident.

An important first step in the reconstruction process would be to estimate the position of the pedestrian and the vehicle at selected times before impact. Events of particular importance would include the time before impact at which the pedestrian stepped into the street, and the time at which the pedestrian crossed into the travel lane of the oncoming vehicle. A critical question would be, for each of these two events, did a line of sight exist for the pedestrian to view the headlights of the oncoming vehicle?

Using the previous example (pedestrian 4 feet per second coming from the left and vehicle 40 mph), the low beam headlight intensity in the direction of the pedestrian would be on the order of 500 candela (lumens per steradian) as viewed from a height of 5.5 feet above ground level at the pedestrian position. Assuming a headlight area of 0.25 square feet, this would mean the luminance of the headlight would be on the order of 637 foot-Lamberts. The headlights would be highly visible to the pedestrian provided an unobstructed line of sight exists. By comparison, the illumination of the upper portion of the pedestrian at a distance of 164 feet would be on the order of 0.02 foot-candles. With white clothing (85 percent reflectance) this translates into a pedestrian luminance of 0.017 foot-Lamberts, and with black clothing (10 percent reflectance), 0.002 foot-Lamberts. This means the headlights, viewed from the pedestrian location, are at least 37,470 times the luminance of the pedestrian (white clothing) as viewed from the driver's location.

In the previous example it was assumed that impact took place with the pedestrian 2 feet to the right of the driver's position. Assume that was 4 feet to the right of the lane line. With the pedestrian traveling at a speed of 2.72 miles per hour (4 feet per second) that means the pedestrian entered the vehicle's lane of travel 1 second before impact. With the vehicle traveling at 30 miles per hour (44 feet per second), the vehicle is 44 feet from the point of impact at the time that the pedestrian enters the vehicle's lane of travel. This is a couple of car lengths. Had the pedestrian looked to the right before entering the vehicle's lane of travel, the oncoming vehicle would have been clearly visible and, if the pedestrian had paused before entering the lane to let the vehicle pass, the accident would not have taken place.

3.6 Comparison of Driver and Pedestrian Visual Tasks in Mid-Block Crossings

As stated at the beginning of this chapter, every accident deserves to be analyzed on its own merits without generalization as to where the fault lies. The variables used in the example were not intended to suggest that pedestrians are always at fault, but rather to point out the dramatic differences that can occur with respect to the level of difficulty of the visual tasks for the driver and for the pedestrian.

Pedestrians, making a mid-block crossing, need to recognize that they do not have the right-of-way, and it is therefore in their best interests to see that the crossing can be made safely. Pedestrians, looking into a bright pair of headlights, may make poor judgments as to the oncoming vehicle speed and distance, and/or overestimate their own visibility and assume that the driver will see them and take necessary action to avoid an accident.

3.7 Pedestrians Making Intersection Crossings in Crosswalks with Streetlights

An intersection with marked or unmarked crosswalks creates a different environment in that a vehicle driver should be expecting that there might be pedestrian crossings in progress. This imposes on the driver the need to perform a visual search for pedestrians during the intersection approach.

Most of the pedestrian-vehicle accidents in crosswalks the author has encountered have occurred at night. For an intersection without streetlights, the vehicle headlights and their effectiveness is as described in discussing the mid-block pedestrian crossing. However, in an intersection with streetlights, these lights might be expected to provide the dominant lighting.

3.8 Intersection Lighting Provided by Streetlights

There is a remarkable amount of detailed information on lighting supplied by the Illuminating Engineering Society of North America in its *Lighting Handbook*.[3] This includes numerical data with respect to street lighting including such topics as uniformity of pavement luminance, avoidance of glare, and so on. Our interest in street lighting is primarily directed toward the extent to which the streetlights provide lighting that assists in achieving pedestrian safety. For that specific interest, it is not uniformity of pavement illumination that matters, but rather, the level of illumination of those surfaces where the pedestrian will be viewed by a driver approaching the intersection. The simulated intersection overhead view shown in Figure 3.6 was constructed using three-dimensional animation software.

The cylindrical "pedestrian" used previously is located in this overhead view at the center of the intersection. In terms of uniform illumination of the street, this would appear to be a "well lit" intersection. However, the important question with respect to the intersection lighting has to do with how well a pedestrian in one of the crosswalks is illuminated from the perspective of the driver of an automobile approaching the intersection. In this simulation, north is to the top of the picture. The single streetlight providing the intersection illumination is located on the northeast corner of the intersection with the lamp itself located at a height of approximately 30 feet and extending diagonally into the street (southwest) by approximately 5 feet. The pole on which the streetlight is mounted is visible in

Figure 3.6 *Computer-generated overhead view of an intersection illuminated by a single streetlight.*

this overhead view. In this simplified example, there is no significant background illumination in any of the four directions leading away from the intersection.

In some residential areas, it is common to see many intersections illuminated by a single streetlight. The simulation is intended to illustrate such an intersection with one lane of traffic in each direction and painted crosswalks on all four pedestrian entries to the intersection. To complete the simulation, "cameras" were located 3.5 feet above ground level, 120 feet from the center of the intersection, in all four directions of vehicle approach to give a driver-view. It should be emphasized that the numerical values used for this simulated example are for the purpose of illustrating some fundamental concepts, and each real world accident must be judged based on the specific circumstances involved. The simplified cylindrical model of a "pedestrian" previously described, rather than a more

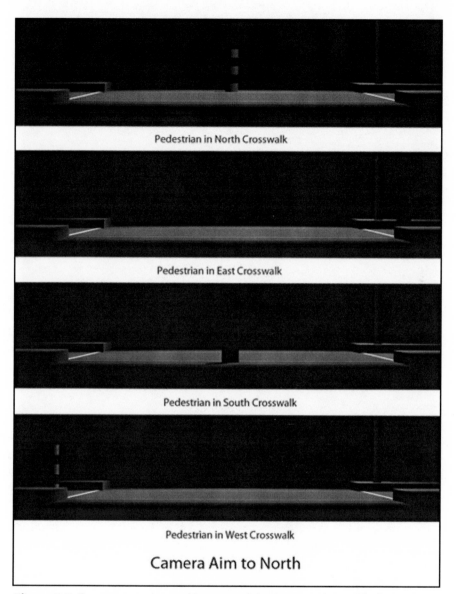

Figure 3.7 *Computer-animated images of the intersection with the camera located to the south of the intersection and aimed to the north. Each of the four images shows the cylindrical target located in one of the four crosswalks.*

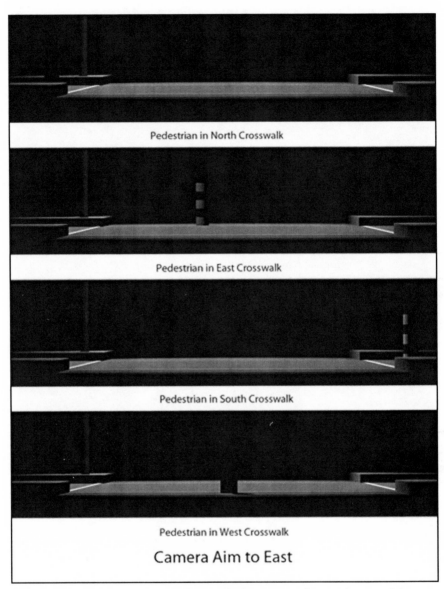

Pedestrian in North Crosswalk

Pedestrian in East Crosswalk

Pedestrian in South Crosswalk

Pedestrian in West Crosswalk

Camera Aim to East

Figure 3.8 Same as Figure 3.7 but with the camera located west of the intersection and aimed to the east.

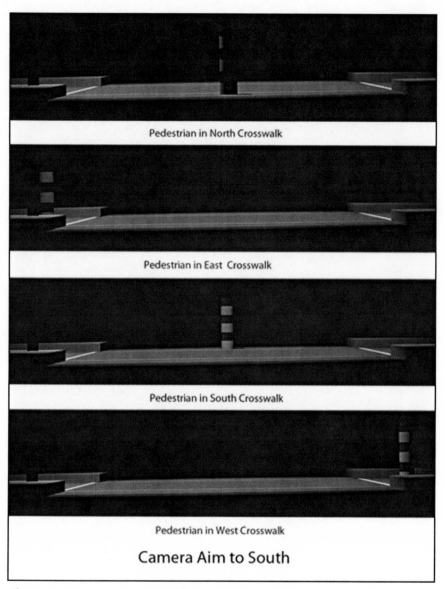

Figure 3.9 *Same as Figure 3.7 but with the camera located north of the intersection and aimed to the south.*

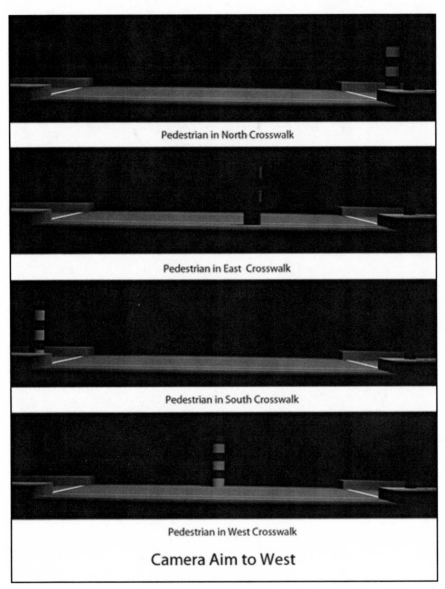

Figure 3.10 Same as Figure 3.7 but with the camera located east of the intersection and aimed to the west.

realistic three-dimensional model of a pedestrian, is used so that the specifics of the attire, skin tone, and so on, would not bias the basic concepts of the problems associated with streetlight illumination. Figure 3.7 is a set of four views from the camera located to the south of the intersection and pointed to the north. Each view shows the "pedestrian" located in one of the four crosswalks. Figures 3.8, 3.9 and 3.10 are similar, showing the view from each of the other three cameras.

The purpose of showing these four figures is to demonstrate the importance of the directionality of the lighting. There are two aspects of the illumination directionality. Many of the combinations of camera, streetlight, and "pedestrian" positions create situations such that the primary surfaces of the "pedestrian" visible to the driver are not well illuminated. But the second important factor is that for those surfaces that are illuminated, the luminance depends upon the angle of the illumination with respect to the orientation of each surface. Mathematically, the luminance of a diffuse surface is dependent upon the product of the illumination level in foot-candles times the reflectance of the surface, times the cosine of the angle between the direction of the illumination and the perpendicular to the surface. Maximum luminance is achieved when the illumination is perpendicular to the surface. Zero luminance results from illumination that is at grazing incidence, that is, at 90 degrees with respect to the perpendicular. Figure 3.11 illustrates the illumination levels that are achieved as a function of the direction from which the light arrives relative to the perpendicular to the horizontal surface.

If the horizontal surface is a roadway, then the maximum roadway luminance is achieved with a streetlamp located directly over the surface. However, such lighting will be ineffective in illuminating the vertical surfaces of a pedes-

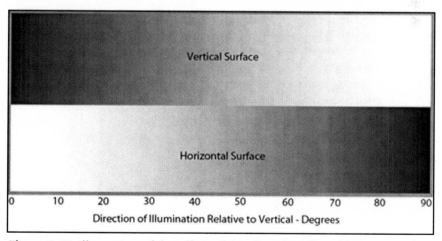

Figure 3.11 *Illustration of the effect of the directionality of lighting on the resulting illumination.*

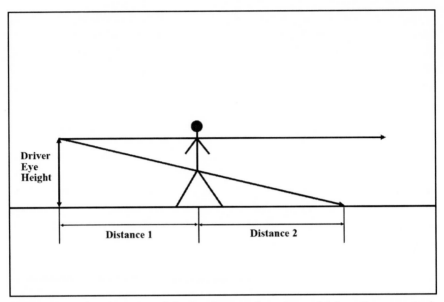

Figure 3.12 *The distance of the background against which various vertical portions of a pedestrian would be viewed by an approaching motorist.*

trian. If the illumination of both the roadway and the pedestrian vertical surfaces is at a 45-degree angle, both the roadway and the pedestrian will have luminance values approximately 71 percent of that which would exist if the illumination were perpendicular to each surface.

There may be accident situations where the background against which the pedestrian is viewed is brightly illuminated. In such cases a poorly illuminated pedestrian may be visible as a negative contrast.

A well-illuminated intersection would provide a background that made a darkly clothed pedestrian visible. Figure 3.12 is a sketch showing the line of sight from the driver's eye to the pedestrian and then continued on to the background against which that portion of the pedestrian will be viewed. As a numerical example, assume that the driver's eye height is 4 feet above ground level. The line of sight from the driver to the pedestrian 4 feet above ground level will continue on to infinity at 4 feet above ground level. A line of sight from the driver striking the pedestrian 2 feet above ground level will continue on such that Distance 2 will be equal to Distance 1.

This means that the line of sight will terminate at ground level at a distance from the pedestrian equal to Distance 1. A line of sight from the driver striking the pedestrian 3 feet above ground level will continue on such that Distance 2 will be equal to two times Distance 1. This means that the line of sight will terminate at ground level at a distance from the pedestrian equal to three times Distance 1. To further the example, assume that the vehicle speed is 30 miles per hour (44 feet per second). During a perception-reaction time of 1.5 seconds, the vehicle will travel 66 feet. A panic stop (brakes locked) would take about 2 seconds, during which the vehicle would travel another 44 feet for a total distance of 110 feet. This is the distance at which the sighting must be initiated to brake to a complete stop before hitting the pedestrian. If the driver performs a stop with one-half of the deceleration of a panic stop it will take twice as long (4 seconds) with a stopping distance of 88 feet, so that the total perception-reaction-braking distance is now 154 feet with a sighting of the pedestrian beginning 5.5 seconds before impact. Going back to Figure 3.12, if Distance 1 is 154 feet then the line of sight to the pedestrian 3 feet above ground level will terminate at a distance 308 feet beyond the pedestrian. The line of sight to the pedestrian 2 feet above ground level will terminate 154 feet beyond the pedestrian. For a residential intersection with one lane of travel in each direction, both of these distances are well beyond the dimensions of the intersection. The point to this is that, even if the streetlight provides a uniform illumination of the roadway and crosswalks, the lighted pavement will not be the background of importance against which the pedestrian will be viewed. This is consistent with the observation of pedestrian background in Figures 3.7 through 3.10. The other important factor to take into consideration is that 5.5 seconds before impact with a pedestrian average speed of 4 feet per second, the pedestrian would be 22 feet from impact when the sighting initiating the perception-reaction-braking needs to take place. This means that, depending upon the geometry of the street, the pedestrian may not yet have entered the street when the perception-reaction-braking action needs to begin. There will be pedestrian-vehicle accidents in which the vehicle driver is clearly at fault. But it is essential that the conditions outlined in the previous paragraphs be taken into consideration before making such a judgment. It is also extremely important that pedestrians, in the interest of their own safety and independent of right of way, adopt a defensive mode, carefully observing oncoming vehicles, and never crossing their paths of travel unless there is clear evidence that the vehicle is coming to a stop.

3.9 Food for Thought—Streetlights

The author has no expertise with respect to the many factors that determine the financial aspects associated with street lighting. However, here are a few thoughts on the subject in the hope that they might stimulate someone familiar with these topics to see opportunities for improvement. The author's encounters with street lighting have been primarily associated with automobile/pedestrian accidents. With respect to providing good illumination of pedestrians, pole mounted lights located at corners of intersections are not very effective. There are many types of crosswalk lighting systems. Some have lights imbedded in the pavement outlining the crosswalk; some have flashing lights activated by pedestrian switch pushing or motion sensor devices. Lights imbedded in the pavement on either side of the crosswalk offer the opportunity to illuminate both sides of the pedestrian. With driver familiarity, flashing light systems provide a clear warning of pedestrian activity, even under conditions in which the pedestrian is of low visibility. Despite the maintenance costs, clearly the technique provides good pedestrian illumination and/or warning of pedestrian presence. Also, since the crosswalks represent only a small percentage of the intersection, the light power required for intersection illumination is substantially reduced with systems that illuminate only the crosswalks. With respect to total power requirements, motion sensors that activate the lighting only when there is activity could dramatically reduce the total power used. For example, many streetlights remain on from dusk to dawn. However, the percentage of time during which there is any activity warranting such illumination is minuscule.

3.10 Pedestrian Trip/Slip and Fall Accidents

There are many types of trip/slip and fall accidents. This section is limited to the specific types of accidents to which the author has been exposed. Walking can be viewed as a series of interrupted falls. The center of gravity of the human body is generally located at approximately 55 percent of body height. Walking begins by leaning forward so that the center of gravity moves forward, ahead of our feet. Once that happens, if nothing is done to prevent a continuation of that movement, our bodies will be carried to the ground. What we do to stop the downward movement is to move one of our legs forward so that our foot comes in contact with the ground ahead of the center of gravity and the fall is prevented. This is followed by continued leaning forward with the fall again interrupted by the movement of our other leg, placing that foot in contact with the ground ahead of the center of gravity. One type of fall involves the rear foot encountering some kind of an obstacle so that its forward movement is prevented. A very small "ridge" can prevent that foot from moving forward thus resulting in a fall. Another type of fall involves a situation in which the foot that is moved forward does not encounter a stable, flat surface and therefore is unable to stop the forward and downward rotation of the body.

3.11 Rule for Safe Walking

There may very well be situations in which a pedestrian has the right to expect that the path of travel will be free from obstacles that may result in a fall. That is a legal issue, outside of the scope of this book. Setting aside questions of fault, pedestrians need to adopt a defensive mode with the desire to protect themselves from personal injury generated by a fall. To accomplish this objective, pedestrians must be able to sight the path ahead in order to be able to visually determine whether the surface where they will be placing their foot during their next step forward is conducive to stability. Achieving this result may require a reduction in walking speed. If the visibility conditions are such that an accurate judgment cannot be made, then there is a definite possibility that a fall may occur. Under favorable visibility conditions, a visual clearance of the path of travel may be directed some distance ahead so that only an occasional downward look is required. Under the poorest of visibility conditions, a continuous downward look may be required, and, in the worst-case scenario, walking safely may actually require a shuffling ahead with the forward foot, physically, rather than visually, testing out the surface conditions.

3.12 Types of Trip/Slip and Fall Accidents

In numerous cases investigated, it was apparent that the object or defect that caused the fall would have been clearly visible, if the involved party had been looking down along the future path of travel. Where we point our eyes is dictated by a mental priority list of what is important to see in our current environment. We can be attracted by interesting scenery, other people of interest, and so on. When that happens, we are likely to end up violating the rules for safe walking. Photographs, properly captured and displayed, can demonstrate the visibility of the aspects of the scene that could lead to a slip and fall.

Accidents involving stairways are common. Inadequate lighting can be an important factor. Another frequently occurring problem involves steps that have no pattern structure. When descending on a frontally lighted stairway, there will be no visible shadow pattern cast by the steps and no view of the riser between steps. With this type of situation, it can be virtually impossible to visually determine where one step ends and the next step begins. Taping or painting the leading edge of each step with a reflectance and color sharply different than the step surface can dramatically improve the situation. Handrails on the stairway can minimize the chances of a fall even when a misstep does occur.

Other accidents include tripping on an asphalt gouge in a commercial parking lot area and tripping over a wheel stop in a parking area. In these kinds of cases, while experts can testify as to whether or not the accident party should have been able to see and avoid the accident, photographic evidence, properly collected and presented, offers the best opportunity to make the visibility issues apparent to the viewer.

3.13 Vehicle/Vehicle Accidents
A. Types of Vehicle/Vehicle Accidents

The author's experience with vehicle/vehicle accidents have included rear-end collisions, crossing or turning in the presence of oncoming traffic, multiple collisions involving unlit stationary vehicles in the roadway, and an occasional "moth to the flame" encounter in which a driver steers off the roadway into a well lit stationary vehicle parked alongside the roadway. These accidents raise issues as to the driver's capabilities and limitations with respect to making reliable estimates of the other vehicle's distance, speed, and path of travel from the visual cues available. These matters are addressed in the following sections.

3.14 Distance Judgment

Estimates of the distance of an object can be made in a number of ways. The visual system has some basic properties that can aid in making distance estimates for targets at short distance. These include accommodation (focus of the eye), convergence (the toeing in of the two eyes), and stereopsis (separation of the two eyes making the two views slightly different). However, the benefits of accommodation and stereopsis are limited to very short distances. For greater distances, distance judgments are made on the basis of the "angular size" of an object compared with estimates of its actual size, and/or the position of the object relative to other features viewed in the scene.

Asking eyewitnesses for distance estimates is a risky endeavor. Asking for distances in terms of car lengths may be better than estimates in feet; however, there is still likely to be substantial error by many eyewitnesses. One reason is that distance estimation skill has to be based on practice in making estimates followed by determining the actual distance. Without experiencing the second half of that sentence, we never learn to appreciate the direction and magnitude of our estimate errors and therefore never improve. As an example of an individual that can produce accurate estimates, a police officer, trained in accident investigation and reconstruction, testified that, throughout his career, he has made a habit of estimating distances at accident sites and then immediately following this up with a direct measurement. This officer can undoubtedly produce better distance estimations than those who have not undergone that type of training.

3.15 Eyewitness Testimony

There are several excellent publications dealing with the reliability of eyewitness testimony.[4,5] The author has encountered a sizeable number of examples of clearly unreliable eyewitness testimony. One such accident involved an intersection collision that was witnessed by a driver approaching the intersection. The witness did not know either of the parties involved in the accident, and appeared to have no bias as to who was at fault. He was interviewed by the police officer investigating the accident and was then called as a witness in the trial, which took place a considerable period of time after the accident. In the course of his trial examination he was asked how fast he was travelling at the time of the collision. He said that his speed was about 20 miles per hour. The attorney then reminded him that the police report indicated he was travelling about 35 miles per hour. He responded that he could not have been travelling that fast because he had been stopped at the stop sign at the preceding intersection and was just accelerating forward at the time of the accident. However, the attorney then pointed out that the stop sign was installed 1 year after the accident. Further examination revealed that the witness travelled that route every morning on his way to work. When he found that he was going to be called to testify, he attempted to refresh his memory of the details of the accident day as he drove to work each day a year after the accident.

In another example, an eyewitness to an intersection accident gave a detailed description of the accident. She was asked about the lighting at the time of the accident and responded that there was good lighting with the sun well up in the sky. Actually, the accident took place about a half-hour after sunset.

In a nighttime accident the driver of a vehicle left the highway and crashed into a well-lit vehicle parked in a dirt area off the roadway. In an interview by the police at the scene and in a second interview several weeks later, the driver said he had no idea how this accident had happened. However, by the time of his deposition and trial testimony, he gave a detailed description of the accident, including the fact that there was a high-speed vehicle approaching him in his lane of travel, and that he had no recourse but to get off the roadway.

When we are involved in a significant event, like an accident, we have a strong desire to try to understand how things happened. As a result, we can undergo a process of "mental reconstruction" in which we try hard to make sense of the events involved. This may start by thinking, "Maybe this is what happened," and if that "maybe" seems to offer a plausible explanation, then over a period of time it becomes more solid every time we bring it up from memory, and finally it becomes, "This is the way it happened."

It is important to understand that, unlike a digital camera, we do not store images. What we do place in our memory is our interpretation of what we believe are important details that we derive from our visual sightings. Each time we pull these events from memory and study them, we may refine our interpretations and end up adding detail not present in our original stored memory. Following that mental activity, we will once again store the information in memory and this updated memory will incorporate these new interpretations and details that were not previously recorded.

3.16 Sensing Closure

When two objects are on a potential collision course, the action taken by one or both parties may be based upon mental estimates of the rapidity with which closure is taking place. An important example would include a driver making a left turn on a roadway based on making a judgment as to whether there is time to do so with safe clearance from a vehicle approaching in the opposite direction. Another example is the situation involved in encountering slow-moving or stationary vehicles on the highway where it is not immediately apparent to the approaching driver that the distance between the two vehicles is decreasing rapidly and action is required. There are a number of ways in which closure can be sensed. One of the simpler situations is that in which the target object is viewed relative to some other object in the scene, for example a vehicle that is stationary in the vicinity of an intersection, so that the driver can observe that the vehicle is not changing position with respect to the crossing roadway and is therefore stationary. On a dark night with an open roadway, where those kinds of physical reference points may not exist, closure is generally sensed by noting that the angular "size" of the object is increasing. The growth of the size implies closure. There are again, two different types of motion sensing. Viewing a clock with a minute hand and a second hand is one way of visualizing these two types. If we view the minute hand, it will not be immediately apparent that there is any movement. If we continue to stare at the minute hand, we will eventually see that it has changed positions with respect to the clock face. This might be termed "static" motion detection. On the other hand, if we view the second hand, it is almost instantaneously evident that it is in motion. This can be termed "dynamic" motion detection. Applied to the roadway situation, we may recall that we first saw a tractor-trailer off in the distance and then later recognize that it is now significantly closer. This is an example of static motion detection. As we get closer

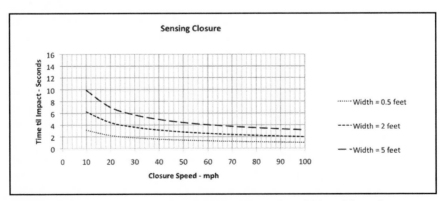

Figure 3.13 *Time until impact at which a driver would be able to begin to sense closure as a function of closure speed for three different target widths.*

to the trailer a point will be reached where it is "instantaneously" apparent it is getting larger, that is, we are closing. Experiments have demonstrated that the threshold for dynamic sensing of image motion takes place when the angular size of an object is growing by approximately 0.003 radians per second.[6] This does not mean that an accurate estimate of closure speed can be made at that point, but simply that we become aware that some level of closure is taking place. Figure 3.13 is a graph showing calculations of the time before impact at which closure can begin to be sensed as a function of the closure speed and the physical dimensions of the target. The "5 feet" example is a typical separation of a pair of automobile taillights. The "2 feet" example came from an accident involving a motorcycle that had multiple headlights, the outer two of which were separated by 2 feet. The "0.5 feet" came from an accident involving a motorcycle with a single headlight, approximately 6 inches in diameter.

3.17 Following Distance

There is an unwritten rule in Los Angeles that, if you leave a two-car length space between your vehicle and the vehicle directly ahead, you will quickly find that two new vehicles will have filled that gap. What is a safe following distance under normal freeway driving conditions? An important aspect of answering that question has to do with the perception-reaction time involved. While numerical values of perception-reaction time are frequently quoted in accident analysis, it is in fact a very complex matter. For an excellent discussion of the various factors that make it difficult to reliably offer a specific number, see Dr. Paul Olson's excellent and thorough discussion of the subject.[7] For those involved in the analysis of accidents, it is very convenient to accept commonly quoted perception-reaction times, such as 1.5 seconds for most situations or as high as 2.5 seconds for more complex and unexpected encounters. Perhaps it would be beneficial to perform our analyses with three different perception-reaction times, as for example, 0.75, 1.5, and 3.0 seconds. If conclusions as to fault in an accident are different for each of these choices of a perception-reaction time, then caution would need to be exercised in making judgments as to fault.

Following a lead vehicle in heavy traffic would appear to be a reasonably simple type of encounter. Assume the vehicle directly ahead applies full braking and comes to a complete stop. In order to avoid a collision, the driver of the following vehicle needs to apply full brakes when the front bumper of her vehicle is located at the position of the rear bumper of the lead vehicle at the time the lead vehicle's brakes were first applied. This would mean that the two vehicles would reach a stopped position, bumper to bumper, assuming that the braking for each vehicle involves the same coefficient of friction. If we assume a lead vehicle speed of 65 mph, and a perception-reaction time of 1.5 seconds then the following distance would be 143 feet (about 7 car lengths). This is considerably greater spacing than what is seen on the freeways. Even with such a following distance, to avoid a collision, the foot of the driver of the following vehicle needs to be on the brake pedal 1.5 seconds after the brake lights come on.

However, the analysis is not that simple. For example, where were the following vehicle driver's eyes pointed at the time the brake lights came on? A 1 second diversion to the right, to the left, or to the instrument panel is certainly a possibility. That could mean that the brake lights may have been on for 1 second before the driver's perception-reaction process begins. This suggests that collision avoidance requires that the following driver maintain a following distance greater than the perception-reaction time distance and never take his eyes off of the lead vehicle. A further complication is that the brake lights do not indicate how hard the lead driver is pushing on the brake pedal. Our driving experience generally suggests that, for most driving situations, it will be a light braking rather than a full emergency braking and, therefore, light braking is most likely to be the following driver's first response. The initially light braking will need to be followed by another perception-reaction process in which the driver must be able to perceive that the closure rate indicates that the lead vehicle is doing more than a light braking and that the response needs to be a switch to a heavy braking if a collision is to be avoided. The question would be, how long will that process take?

3.18 Importance of Signal Lights

Signal lights are of great importance because they allow drivers to recognize other vehicles' intended actions long before those actions themselves can be visually detected. Turn signals are a good example. The author has investigated a number of accidents in which the drivers have stated that they did not use turn signals because they were unaware of the presence of the other vehicle. It is for this reason that the use of turn signals should be an automatic process for each and every turn. Some drivers tend to delay engaging the turn signal until just before the turn is initiated, thus negating the advance warning that can be of such great importance in the prevention of collisions. Four-way flashers are extremely valuable in alerting other vehicles to the presence of a slow-moving or stationary vehicle long before that fact can be deduced from visual observation. And, of course, brake lights alert other vehicles that the brakes are being applied well before there is useful visual evidence derived from being able to sense a change in closure.

3.19 Unlit Stationary Vehicles at Night

An unlit, stopped vehicle on a roadway at night creates an extremely dangerous situation, frequently leading to collisions, sometimes multiple, with oncoming traffic. The driver of such a vehicle should make every effort to activate the emergency flashers. Some new vehicles have the capability of sensing a collision and automatically activate the emergency flashers. Visual sighting of a stationary vehicle is made by virtue of the brake lights/emergency flashers, taillights, headlight illumination of retroreflectors, or headlight illumination of the vehicle body. Figure 3.14 illustrates the dramatic differences between the luminance associated with these alternative sources as a function of the viewing distance.

Assuming favorable atmospheric visibility conditions, the luminance of brake lights or taillights do not change with distance. They do become smaller angular size targets with increase in viewing distance, but it is common experience that either of these light sources are easily visible for distances well beyond the 500 feet shown in the chart. By contrast the luminance of the vehicle body paint surfaces are dependent upon headlight illumination, which decreases with the square of the distance. For the 5 to 1 distance range shown in the chart, this corresponds to a 25 to 1 reduction in illumination with a corresponding 25 to 1 reduction in luminance. In that regard, it may seem surprising to see that, in the example shown, the retroreflector luminance decreases by a smaller factor than that of the white or black auto surface luminance values. To understand this, it is necessary to discuss the way in which retroreflectors function.

A diffuse reflecting material such as a sheet of non-glossy white paper has a reflectance close to unity, meaning that virtually all of the light striking the surface is reflected in all directions into the surrounding hemisphere. By contrast, a retroreflector is structured such that a ray of light striking the reflector encounters

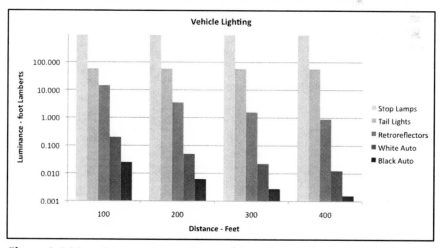

Figure 3.14 Luminance comparison at four selected distances of stop lamps, taillights, retroreflectors, and vehicle body paint.

multiple internal reflections such that the ray of light is sent back close to the direction from which it came. The "observation angle" is defined as the angle that separates the line from the light source to the retroreflector and the line from the retroreflector to the eye of the observer. For an observer located close to the light source, the retroreflector will have a luminance much greater than that of a white high reflectance diffuse surface. By contrast, an observer located a substantial observation angle from the light source will receive very little return and the retroreflector will appear to be quite dark. The reflectance is equal to the luminance of the surface (foot Lamberts) divided by the illumination of the surface (foot candles). There are two compensating factors involved in determining the retroreflector luminance. The first is that the amount of headlight illumination falling on the retroreflector will decrease with the square of the distance which acts in the direction of decreasing the luminance. By contrast, for a given separation distance between the light source and the eye of the observer, the observation angle will decrease with an increase in distance from the retroreflector which increases the luminance. The luminance values for the retroreflector shown in Figure 3.14 assume a headlight/eye separation of 1.5 feet, which is the value for the left headlamp and an exemplar eye height in an exemplar vehicle. The retroreflector data was calculated from tests performed to determine the reflectance of the retroreflector as a function of the observation angle. It is of interest to note that the luminance of the retroreflector changes by a factor of only about 2.3 to 1 over the distance range of 100 to 500 feet, whereas the headlight illumination decreases by a factor of 25 to 1. The retroreflector used for these tests was white. A red retroreflector would produce a lower luminance by a factor of approximately 4 to 1.

The calculations assumed a low beam headlight with an intensity of 3000 candela in a straight ahead direction. The overall range of luminance values is so large that, when graphing the data, it is necessary to use a logarithmic scale to allow the lower values to be seen. Visually this tends to minimize the impression of these dramatic differences. For that reason, the numerical values are listed rather than showing them graphically.

Luminance Values (foot Lamberts)

Distance (Feet)	Brake Light	Taillights	Retroreflectors	White Vehicle	Black Vehicle
100	955	57	4.09	0.240	0.030
200	955	57	6.08	0.060	0.0075
300	955	57	3.95	0.027	0.0033
400	955	57	2.56	0.015	0.0019
500	955	57	1.77	0.0096	0.0012

It is clear from these numerical results that retroreflectors are no substitute for brakelights or taillights. The retroreflectors do play an important role in accidents in which unlit vehicles end up in the roadway. This is demonstrated by noting the difference in luminance between the retroreflectors and the unlit, white or black vehicles. At 100 feet distance the white retroreflector luminance is approximately 17 times the luminance of a white vehicle and 136 times the luminance of a black vehicle. A red retroreflector would be approximately five times the luminance of a white vehicle and 34 times the luminance of a black vehicle. Because of the decrease in "observation angle" with distance, these ratios increase with distance so that at 500 feet distance, the white retroreflector has 184 times the luminance of a white vehicle and 1,475 times the luminance of a black vehicle.

3.20 Disability Glare

When a driver is preparing to make a turn in front of an oncoming vehicle, disability glare can affect judgment regarding sufficient time for a safe completion of the turn. Disability glare is the result of scattering that takes place in the lens system of the eye including those that are due to defects in the lens that will generally increase with age. The net result is that bright light sources, such as headlights, will have a "halo" surrounding the image. The following equation provides a numerical approximation[4] to the luminance values associated with this "halo" for a normal eye:

$$B(G) = 9.3*pi*E/(Theta*(Theta+1.5)), \qquad \text{Eq 3.1}$$

Where B(G) is the disability glare luminance in foot-Lamberts, E is the illumination in foot-candles at the pupil of the eye from the glare source, and Theta is the angle in degrees from the glare source. Looking ahead down the roadway toward an oncoming low beam headlight (2500 cd), Figure 3.15 is a graph showing the numerical values of the disability glare.

Looking back at the luminance values presented in Figure 3.14, at a distance of 100 feet, the glare luminance 2 degrees away from the glare source (approximately 1 foot Lambert) would be five times the luminance of a white automobile illuminated by low-beam headlights and 40 times the luminance of a black automobile. Two degrees at a distance of 100 feet is approximately 3.5 feet. So the disability glare would be another factor tending to mask out any detail associated with the oncoming vehicle other than the headlight itself. A dramatic example involved a driver wanting to make a turn while facing a number of oncoming headlights. Due to the combined limitations of closure sensing and disability glare, the driver was unable to see the scene detail that would have made it possible to determine that one of the headlights was that of a motorcycle approaching at high speed.

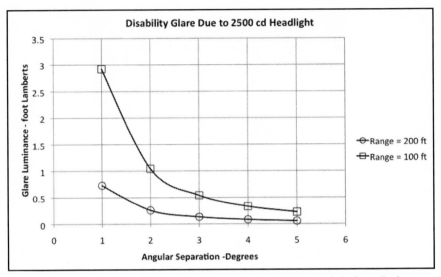

Figure 3.15 *Disability glare calculations for a 2500 candela headlight viewed at 100 and 200 feet as a function of angular separation from the headlight direction.*

Endnotes

1. A Policy on Geometric Design of Highways and Streets, American Association of State Highway and Transportation Officials, 1984, p. 114

2. Western Washington University Planetarium. Accessed 10/25/11 from http://www.wwu.edu/skywise/twilight.html.

3. The IESNA Lighting Handbook, Ninth Edition, Library of Congress Catalog Number 99-76610.

4. Robins, Patrick J., *Eyewitness Reliability in Motor Vehicle Accident Reconstruction and Litigation, Second Edition*. Lawyers & Judges Publishing, 2009.

5. Loftus, Elizabeth F, Eyewitness Testimony, Harvard University Press, 1996.

6. Hoffman, Errol R. and Rudolf G. Mortimer, Scaling of Relative Velocity Between Vehicles, Accident Analysis and Prevention, Vol. 28, No. 4, pp 415-421, 1996.

7. Olson, Paul L., Robert Dewar and Eugene Farber. *Forensic Aspects of Driver Perception and Response, Third Edition*. Lawyers & Judges Publishing, 2010.

Chapter 4

Aircraft Accidents

4.1 Midair Collisions

The primary visibility issues associated with midair collisions involve the extent to which each pilot would have been able to extract information from visual sightings that would have allowed for successful evasive action to avoid the collision. It is also important to examine the information available to an air traffic controller by means of visual observations to determine whether this would have been sufficient to alert the pilots to a potential threat and/or issue alterations in flight paths, which would have prevented a collision.

4.2 Flight Path Analysis

The first step in analyzing the visibility aspects of a midair collision is to locate each of the aircraft involved and their orientation with respect to each other. The primary source for developing this information is the radar data that has been collected. The raw data consists of range, azimuth, and altitude as a function of time. It is important to take into consideration the limitations in accuracy associated with this data. The range values are expressed in nautical miles from the radar to the aircraft and rounded to $^1/_8$ nautical miles. The azimuth from the radar to the target aircraft is recorded in terms of azimuth change pulse counts (ACP's) where 4,096 ACP's = 360 degrees. Altitude is reported in terms of 100-foot increments above sea level and is generated by a transponder response from the aircraft based upon the aircraft altimeter reading. These three dimensions of radar data accuracy can be used to generate three-dimensional "error boxes." For the purpose of illustrating the processing of the radar data, flight paths are generated here for a pair of aircraft, AC1 and AC2, which end up on a collision course. An arbitrary location is selected for the radar and then generated radar data (range, azimuth, and elevation) that would depict the two flight paths. For the purpose of these calculations, the time between radar hits is assumed to be 4.5 seconds. The corresponding three-dimen-

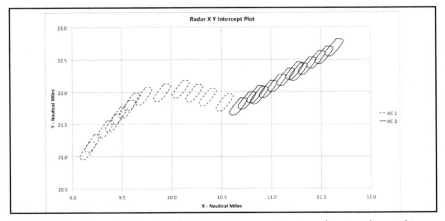

Figure 4.1 *Plot of radar error boxes in X (east-west) and Y (north-south) directions for two aircraft on a collision course.*

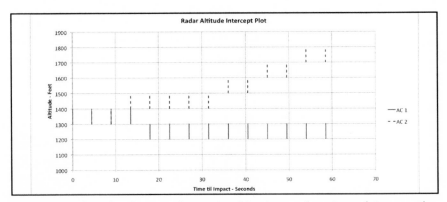

Figure 4.2 *Plot of radar error boxes in altitude as a function of time until impact.*

	A	B	C	D	E	F	G	H	I	J	K	L	M	N	O	P	Q
1	Aircraft 1		Wind														
2			Vel K	Direction					Stall Speed =	49.5	kts						
3			17	270					Cruise Speed	113.0	kts						
4									Aspect Ratio = 6.2								
5			Wind Correction (ft per second)						AOA = AOA(Stall)/(Speed/Stall Speed)^2/cos(Bank)								
6			X	Y					Pitch = AOA - AOA(Cruise) + atan(Climb*60/(V(k)*6076/3600))								
7			29	0					AOA	18.00	deg	Pitch =	14.54	deg			
8			Wind Correction (nm/sec)						AOA	3.46	deg	Pitch =	0.00	deg			
9			X	Y													
10			0	0													
11	Impact at 21:03:50												TRUE				
12	Clock	T	dT	V(k)	dV(k)	C	dC	B	dB	X Calc	Y Calc	Z Calc	H	dH	R	AOA	Pitch
13	21:03:50	0.0		112.00		100		0		10.679	21.805	1327	111.00		0.0	3.52	0.57
14	21:03:50	0.5	0.5	112.00	0.00	100	0	0	0	10.66	21.81	1326	111.00	0.0	0.0	3.52	0.57
15	21:03:49	1.0	0.5	112.00	0.00	100	0	0	0	10.65	21.82	1325	111.00	0.0	0.0	3.52	0.57
16	21:03:49	1.5	0.5	112.00	0.00	100	0	0	0	10.63	21.82	1325	111.00	0.0	0.0	3.52	0.57
17	21:03:48	2.0	0.5	112.00	0.00	100	0	0	0	10.61	21.83	1324	111.00	0.0	0.0	3.52	0.57
18	21:03:48	2.5	0.5	112.00	0.00	100	0	0	0	10.59	21.83	1323	111.00	0.0	0.0	3.52	0.57
19	21:03:47	3.0	0.5	112.00	0.00	100	0	0	0	10.58	21.84	1322	111.00	0.0	0.0	3.52	0.57
20	21:03:47	3.5	0.5	112.00	0.00	100	0	0	0	10.56	21.84	1321	111.00	0.0	0.0	3.52	0.57
21	21:03:46	4.0	0.5	112.00	0.00	100	0	0	0	10.54	21.85	1320	111.00	0.0	0.0	3.52	0.57
22	21:03:46	4.5	0.5	112.00	0.00	100	0	0	0	10.53	21.86	1320	111.00	0.0	0.0	3.52	0.57
23	21:03:45	5.0	0.5	112.00	0.00	100	0	0	0	10.51	21.86	1319	111.00	0.0	0.0	3.52	0.57
24	21:03:45	5.5	0.5	112.00	0.00	100	0	0	0	10.49	21.87	1318	111.00	0.0	0.0	3.52	0.57
25	21:03:44	6.0	0.5	112.00	0.00	100	0	0	0	10.48	21.87	1317	111.00	0.0	0.0	3.52	0.57
26	21:03:44	6.5	0.5	112.00	0.00	100	0	0	0	10.46	21.88	1316	111.00	0.0	0.0	3.52	0.57
27	21:03:43	7.0	0.5	112.00	0.00	100	0	0	0	10.44	21.88	1315	111.00	0.0	0.0	3.52	0.57
28	21:03:43	7.5	0.5	112.00	0.00	100	0	0	0	10.43	21.89	1315	111.00	0.0	0.0	3.52	0.57
29	21:03:42	8.0	0.5	112.00	0.00	100	0	0	0	10.41	21.89	1314	111.00	0.0	0.0	3.52	0.57
30	21:03:42	8.5	0.5	112.00	0.00	100	0	0	0	10.39	21.90	1313	111.00	0.0	0.0	3.52	0.57
31	21:03:41	9.0	0.5	112.00	0.00	100	0	0	0	10.38	21.91	1312	111.00	0.0	0.0	3.52	0.57
32	21:03:41	9.5	0.5	112.00	0.00	100	0	0	0	10.36	21.91	1311	111.00	0.0	0.0	3.52	0.57
33	21:03:40	10.0	0.5	112.00	0.00	100	0	0	0	10.34	21.92	1310	111.00	0.0	0.0	3.52	0.57
34	21:03:40	10.5	0.5	112.00	0.00	100	0	0	0	10.32	21.92	1310	111.00	0.0	0.0	3.52	0.57
35	21:03:39	11.0	0.5	112.00	0.00	100	0	0	0	10.31	21.93	1309	111.00	0.0	0.0	3.52	0.57
36	21:03:39	11.5	0.5	112.00	0.00	100	0	0	0	10.29	21.93	1308	111.00	0.0	0.0	3.52	0.57
37	21:03:38	12.0	0.5	112.00	0.00	100	0	0	0	10.27	21.94	1307	111.00	0.0	0.0	3.52	0.57
38	21:03:38	12.5	0.5	112.00	0.00	100	0	0	0	10.26	21.94	1306	111.00	0.0	0.0	3.52	0.57
39	21:03:37	13.0	0.5	112.00	0.00	100	0	0	0	10.24	21.95	1305	111.00	0.0	0.0	3.52	0.57
40	21:03:37	13.5	0.5	112.00	0.00	100	0	0	0	10.22	21.96	1305	111.00	0.0	0.0	3.52	0.57
41	21:03:36	14.0	0.5	112.00	0.00	100	0	0	0	10.21	21.96	1304	111.00	0.0	0.0	3.52	0.57
42	21:03:36	14.5	0.5	112.00	0.00	100	0	0	0	10.19	21.97	1303	111.00	0.0	0.0	3.52	0.57
43	21:03:35	15.0	0.5	112.00	0.00	100	0	0	0	10.17	21.97	1302	111.00	0.0	0.0	3.52	0.57
44	21:03:35	15.5	0.5	112.00	0.00	100	0	0	0	10.16	21.98	1301	111.00	0.0	0.0	3.52	0.57
45	21:03:34	16.0	0.5	112.00	0.00	100	0	0	0	10.14	21.98	1300	111.00	0.0	0.0	3.52	0.57
46	21:03:34	16.5	0.5	112.00	0.00	100	0	0	0	10.12	21.99	1300	111.00	0.0	0.0	3.52	0.57
47	21:03:33	17.0	0.5	112.00	0.00	100	0	0	0	10.10	21.99	1299	111.00	0.0	0.0	3.52	0.57
48	21:03:33	17.5	0.5	112.00	0.00	100	0	0	0	10.09	22.00	1298	111.00	0.0	0.0	3.52	0.57
49	21:03:32	18.0	0.5	112.00	0.00	100	0	15	15	10.07	22.01	1297	110.35	-0.7	2.6	3.64	0.69
50	21:03:32	18.5	0.5	112.00	0.00	100	0	30	15	10.05	22.01	1296	108.28	-2.1	5.6	4.07	1.11
51	21:03:31	19.0	0.5	112.00	0.00	100	0	30	0	10.04	22.02	1295	105.47	-2.8	5.6	4.07	1.11
52	21:03:31	19.5	0.5	112.00	0.00	100	0	30	0	10.02	22.02	1295	102.65	-2.8	5.6	4.07	1.11
53	21:03:30	20.0	0.5	112.00	0.00	100	0	30	0	10.00	22.02	1294	99.83	-2.8	5.6	4.07	1.11

Figure 4.3 Spreadsheet used to develop an aircraft track, for aircraft 1 on a collision course with aircraft 2, consistent with the radar error boxes.

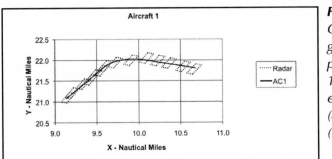

Figure 4.3a
Graph of generated flight path for aircraft 1 through radar error boxes, X (east-west) vs. Y (north-south).

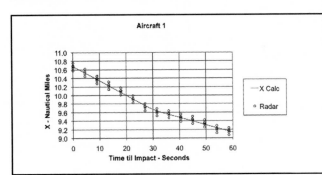

Figure 4.3b
Graph of generated flight path for aircraft 1 through radar error boxes, X (east-west) vs. time to impact.

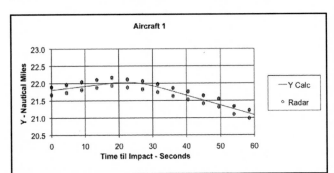

Figure 4.3c
Graph of generated flight path for aircraft 1 through radar error boxes, Y (north-south) vs. time to impact.

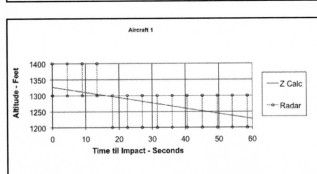

Figure 4.3d
Graph of generated flight path for aircraft 1 through radar error boxes, altitude vs. time to impact.

sional radar error boxes are calculated using an Excel worksheet. Figure 4.1 is a graph showing an X-Y (east-west, north-south) representation of the results. Figure 4.2 is an altitude versus time to impact graph showing the altitude error range.

For Figure 4.2, the next step was to use an Excel worksheet that allows calculation of the details of a flight path for each aircraft that would be consistent with this radar data. Figure 4.3 shows the data generated for Aircraft 1 covering the last 20 seconds before impact. The complete sample worksheet covers a time period of 60 seconds before impact. The worksheet as shown makes calculations starting with the time of impact and moving backwards in time.

The columns in Figure 4.3 are as follows:

Item	Definition
Clock	Time, local or universal
T	Time in seconds until impact
dT	Time interval between calculations
V(k)	Aircraft velocity in knots
dV(k)	Change in velocity in knots
C	Climb rate in feet per minute
dC	Change in climb rate in feet per minute
B	Bank angle in degrees
dB	Change in bank angle in degrees
X Calc	X (east-west) distance from radar reference point in nautical miles
Y Calc	Y (north- south) distance from radar reference point in nautical miles
Z Calc	Altitude in feet
H	Heading in degrees
dH	Change in heading in degrees
R	Heading change per second due to centripetal force of the bank
AOA	Angle of attack calculation
Pitch	Pitch calculation

Item	Cell Entries Row 13
Clock	Clock time at impact
T	Seconds until impact

dT	No entry
V(k)	Speed at impact
dV(k)	No entry
C	Climb rate at impact
dC	No entry
B	Bank angle at impact
dB	No entry
X Calc	X (east west) position in nautical miles at impact
Y Calc	Y (north-south) position in nautical miles at impact
Z Calc	Altitude in feet at impact
H	Heading in degrees at impact
dH	No entry
R	Worksheet will calculate the numerical value
AOA	Worksheet will calculate the numerical value
Pitch	Worksheet will calculate the numerical value

For the benefit of any reader that would like to generate such a worksheet, Appendix A shows the actual equations associated with each of the worksheet cells.

The calculations are initiated by entering, on the first row, rough estimates of velocity, V(k), climb rate, C, bank angle, B, impact location in terms of X (east-west), Y (north-south), and Z (altitude), and the final heading, H at the time of impact. This worksheet will produce calculations of each of these parameters over the entire time period contained on the worksheet. To alter the flight path of the aircraft at any point in time, entries can be made to change the aircraft velocity, climb rate, and bank angle by entering the appropriate values in dV(k), dC, and/or dB. For example, the worksheet indicates that, at 18.5 seconds before impact, Aircraft 1 has a 30 degree bank angle to the right. At 18.0 seconds before impact the bank angle is decreased to 15 degrees to the right and at 17.5 seconds before impact the bank angle is zero. Column "M" shows the corresponding change in heading associated with the bank angle.

To aid the user in generating an appropriate flight path, there are four graphs displayed on the worksheet. The first graph, Figure 4.3a, is a plot of the calculated X versus Y values and incorporates the error boxes for the Aircraft 1 radar data.

The radar data makes it clear that there will be a bank and turn required. With the graph visible on the worksheet, a bank angle change, dB, at a selected time, T, can be entered with the result observed in terms of how well these entries produce a flight path through the radar error boxes. The numerical changes can be reentered until a satisfactory fit is obtained. It is necessary that a valid flight path not only passes through the error boxes, but also does so at the proper time. That is the reason for the additional graphs. Figure 4.3b is a plot of the calculated X (East-West) values as a function of time until impact, along with the four X values that define the four corners of the radar error boxes.

Figure 4.3c is a similar graph plotting the calculated Y (North-South) values as a function of time until impact along with the four Y values that define the four corners of the radar error boxes.

Figure 4.3d is a plot of the Z (Altitude) values along with the altitude upper and lower radar accuracy limits for altitude.

	A	B	C	D	E	F	G	H	I	J	K	L	M	N	O	P	Q
1	Aircraft 2		Wind														
2			Vel Kts	Direction				Stall Speed =		49.5 kts							
3			17	220				Cruise Speed =		113.0 kts							
4								Aspect Ratio = 6.2									
5			Wind Correction (ft per second)					AOA = AOA(Stall)/(Speed/Stall Speed)^2/cos(Bank)									
6			X	Y				Pitch = AOA - AOA(Cruise) + atan(Climb*60/(V(k)*6076/3600))									
7			18.44	21.98				AOA =		18.00 deg		Pitch =	14.54 deg				
8			Wind Correction (nm/sec)					AOA =		3.46 deg		Pitch =	0.00 deg				
9			X	Y													
10			0.003	0.004													
11	Impact at 21:03:50																
12	Clock	T	dT	V(k)	dV(k)	C	dC	B	dB	X Calc	Y Calc	Z Calc	H	dH	R	AOA	Pitch
13	21:03:50	0		91.00		-400		0		10.679	21.805	1327	226.44		0.0	5.33	-0.61
14	21:03:50	0.5	0.5	91.00	0.00	-400	0	0	0	10.69	21.81	1330	226.44	0.0	0.0	5.33	-0.61
15	21:03:49	1	0.5	91.00	0.00	-400	0	0	0	10.69	21.82	1334	226.44	0.0	0.0	5.33	-0.61
16	21:03:49	1.5	0.5	91.00	0.00	-400	0	0	0	10.70	21.83	1337	226.44	0.0	0.0	5.33	-0.61
17	21:03:48	2	0.5	91.00	0.00	-400	0	0	0	10.71	21.83	1340	226.44	0.0	0.0	5.33	-0.61
18	21:03:48	2.5	0.5	91.00	0.00	-400	0	0	0	10.72	21.84	1344	226.44	0.0	0.0	5.33	-0.61
19	21:03:47	3	0.5	91.00	0.00	-400	0	0	0	10.72	21.85	1347	226.44	0.0	0.0	5.33	-0.61
20	21:03:47	3.5	0.5	91.00	0.00	-400	0	0	0	10.73	21.85	1350	226.44	0.0	0.0	5.33	-0.61
21	21:03:46	4	0.5	91.00	0.00	-400	0	0	0	10.74	21.86	1354	226.44	0.0	0.0	5.33	-0.61
22	21:03:46	4.5	0.5	91.00	0.00	-400	0	0	0	10.75	21.87	1357	226.44	0.0	0.0	5.33	-0.61
23	21:03:45	5	0.5	91.00	0.00	-400	0	0	0	10.76	21.87	1360	226.44	0.0	0.0	5.33	-0.61
24	21:03:45	5.5	0.5	91.00	0.00	-400	0	0	0	10.76	21.88	1364	226.44	0.0	0.0	5.33	-0.61
25	21:03:44	6	0.5	91.00	0.00	-400	0	0	0	10.77	21.89	1367	226.44	0.0	0.0	5.33	-0.61
26	21:03:44	6.5	0.5	91.00	0.00	-400	0	0	0	10.78	21.89	1370	226.44	0.0	0.0	5.33	-0.61
27	21:03:43	7	0.5	91.00	0.00	-400	0	0	0	10.79	21.90	1374	226.44	0.0	0.0	5.33	-0.61
28	21:03:43	7.5	0.5	91.00	0.00	-400	0	0	0	10.79	21.91	1377	226.44	0.0	0.0	5.33	-0.61
29	21:03:42	8	0.5	91.00	0.00	-400	0	0	0	10.80	21.92	1380	226.44	0.0	0.0	5.33	-0.61
30	21:03:42	8.5	0.5	91.00	0.00	-400	0	0	0	10.81	21.92	1384	226.44	0.0	0.0	5.33	-0.61
31	21:03:41	9	0.5	91.00	0.00	-400	0	0	0	10.82	21.93	1387	226.44	0.0	0.0	5.33	-0.61
32	21:03:41	9.5	0.5	91.00	0.00	-400	0	0	0	10.82	21.94	1390	226.44	0.0	0.0	5.33	-0.61
33	21:03:40	10	0.5	91.00	0.00	-400	0	0	0	10.83	21.94	1394	226.44	0.0	0.0	5.33	-0.61
34	21:03:40	10.5	0.5	91.00	0.00	-400	0	0	0	10.84	21.95	1397	226.44	0.0	0.0	5.33	-0.61
35	21:03:39	11	0.5	91.00	0.00	-400	0	0	0	10.85	21.96	1400	226.44	0.0	0.0	5.33	-0.61
36	21:03:39	11.5	0.5	91.00	0.00	-400	0	0	0	10.85	21.96	1404	226.44	0.0	0.0	5.33	-0.61
37	21:03:38	12	0.5	91.00	0.00	-400	0	0	0	10.86	21.97	1407	226.44	0.0	0.0	5.33	-0.61
38	21:03:38	12.5	0.5	91.00	0.00	-400	0	0	0	10.87	21.98	1410	226.44	0.0	0.0	5.33	-0.61
39	21:03:37	13	0.5	91.00	0.00	-400	0	0	0	10.88	21.98	1414	226.44	0.0	0.0	5.33	-0.61
40	21:03:37	13.5	0.5	91.00	0.00	0	400	0	0	10.89	21.99	1415	226.44	0.0	0.0	5.33	1.87
41	21:03:36	14	0.5	91.00	0.00	0	0	0	0	10.89	22.00	1415	226.44	0.0	0.0	5.33	1.87
42	21:03:36	14.5	0.5	91.00	0.00	0	0	0	0	10.90	22.01	1415	226.44	0.0	0.0	5.33	1.87
43	21:03:35	15	0.5	91.00	0.00	0	0	0	0	10.91	22.01	1415	226.44	0.0	0.0	5.33	1.87
44	21:03:35	15.5	0.5	91.00	0.00	0	0	0	0	10.92	22.02	1415	226.44	0.0	0.0	5.33	1.87
45	21:03:34	16	0.5	91.00	0.00	0	0	0	0	10.92	22.03	1415	226.44	0.0	0.0	5.33	1.87
46	21:03:34	16.5	0.5	91.00	0.00	0	0	0	0	10.93	22.03	1415	226.44	0.0	0.0	5.33	1.87
47	21:03:33	17	0.5	91.00	0.00	0	0	0	0	10.94	22.04	1415	226.44	0.0	0.0	5.33	1.87
48	21:03:33	17.5	0.5	91.00	0.00	0	0	0	0	10.95	22.05	1415	226.44	0.0	0.0	5.33	1.87
49	21:03:32	18	0.5	91.00	0.00	0	0	0	0	10.95	22.05	1415	226.44	0.0	0.0	5.33	1.87
50	21:03:32	18.5	0.5	91.00	0.00	0	0	0	0	10.96	22.06	1415	226.44	0.0	0.0	5.33	1.87
51	21:03:31	19	0.5	91.00	0.00	0	0	0	0	10.97	22.07	1415	226.44	0.0	0.0	5.33	1.87
52	21:03:31	19.5	0.5	91.00	0.00	0	0	0	0	10.98	22.07	1415	226.44	0.0	0.0	5.33	1.87
53	21:03:30	20	0.5	91.00	0.00	0	0	0	0	10.98	22.08	1415	226.44	0.0	0.0	5.33	1.87

Figure 4.4 Spreadsheet used to develop an aircraft track, for aircraft 2 on a collision course with aircraft 1, consistent with the radar error boxes.

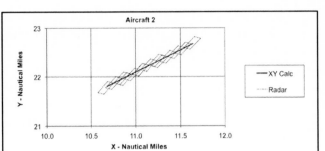

Figure 4.4a
Generated flight path for aircraft 2 through radar error boxes, X (east-west) vs. Y (north-south).

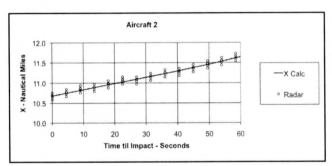

Figure 4.4b
Generated flight path for aircraft 2 through radar error boxes, X (east-west) vs. time to impact.

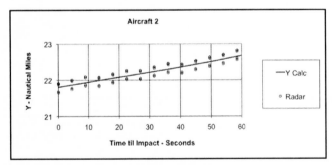

Figure 4.4c
Generated flight path for aircraft 2 through radar error boxes, Y (north-south) vs. time to impact.

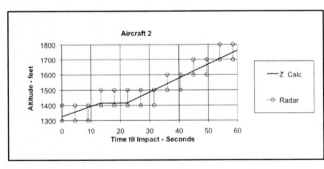

Figure 4.4d
Generated flight path for aircraft 2 through radar error boxes, altitude vs. time to impact.

When the flight path passes through the radar error boxes in all four of these graphs, a flight path consistent with the radar accuracy has been achieved. Figures 4.4 and 4.4a–d are similar output for Aircraft 2.

Figure 4.5 shows the last 20 seconds of another worksheet that takes the generated flight path for the two aircraft and calculates the bearing angles relative to the aircraft axis of the path of sight from Aircraft 1 to Aircraft 2. These calculations take into account the heading, bank, and pitch of Aircraft 1. The three graphs show bearing angle results in terms of 1) azimuth versus elevation, 2) azimuth versus time to impact, and 3) elevation versus time to impact.

	A	B	C	D	E	F	G	H	I	J	K	L	M	N
1	AC1 Bearing Angles to AC2													
2														
3	Time	T	dX	dY	dZ	R(x,y)	AZ0	AZ1	dX	dY	dZ	EL1	AZ2	EL2
4	21:03:50	0.0												
5	21:03:50	0.5	0.025	0.001	4	0.025	86.9	-24.096	-0.010	0.022	4.2	1.599	-24.10	1.03
6	21:03:49	1.0	0.049	0.003	8	0.049	86.9	-24.096	-0.020	0.045	8.3	1.599	-24.10	1.03
7	21:03:49	1.5	0.074	0.004	12	0.074	86.9	-24.096	-0.030	0.067	12.5	1.599	-24.10	1.03
8	21:03:48	2.0	0.098	0.005	17	0.098	86.9	-24.096	-0.040	0.090	16.7	1.599	-24.10	1.03
9	21:03:48	2.5	0.123	0.007	21	0.123	86.9	-24.096	-0.050	0.112	20.8	1.599	-24.10	1.03
10	21:03:47	3.0	0.147	0.008	25	0.147	86.9	-24.096	-0.060	0.135	25.0	1.599	-24.10	1.03
11	21:03:47	3.5	0.172	0.009	29	0.172	86.9	-24.096	-0.070	0.157	29.2	1.599	-24.10	1.03
12	21:03:46	4.0	0.196	0.011	33	0.196	86.9	-24.096	-0.080	0.179	33.3	1.599	-24.10	1.03
13	21:03:46	4.5	0.221	0.012	37	0.221	86.9	-24.096	-0.090	0.202	37.5	1.599	-24.10	1.03
14	21:03:45	5.0	0.245	0.013	42	0.246	86.9	-24.096	-0.100	0.224	41.7	1.599	-24.10	1.03
15	21:03:45	5.5	0.270	0.015	46	0.270	86.9	-24.096	-0.110	0.247	45.8	1.599	-24.10	1.03
16	21:03:44	6.0	0.294	0.016	50	0.295	86.9	-24.096	-0.120	0.269	50.0	1.599	-24.10	1.03
17	21:03:44	6.5	0.319	0.017	54	0.319	86.9	-24.096	-0.130	0.291	54.2	1.599	-24.10	1.03
18	21:03:43	7.0	0.343	0.019	58	0.344	86.9	-24.096	-0.140	0.314	58.3	1.599	-24.10	1.03
19	21:03:43	7.5	0.368	0.020	62	0.368	86.9	-24.096	-0.150	0.336	62.5	1.599	-24.10	1.03
20	21:03:42	8.0	0.392	0.021	67	0.393	86.9	-24.096	-0.160	0.359	66.7	1.599	-24.10	1.03
21	21:03:42	8.5	0.417	0.023	71	0.418	86.9	-24.096	-0.170	0.381	70.8	1.599	-24.10	1.03
22	21:03:41	9.0	0.441	0.024	75	0.442	86.9	-24.096	-0.180	0.404	75.0	1.599	-24.10	1.03
23	21:03:41	9.5	0.466	0.025	79	0.467	86.9	-24.096	-0.191	0.426	79.2	1.599	-24.10	1.03
24	21:03:40	10.0	0.490	0.027	83	0.491	86.9	-24.096	-0.201	0.448	83.3	1.599	-24.10	1.03
25	21:03:40	10.5	0.515	0.028	87	0.516	86.9	-24.096	-0.211	0.471	87.5	1.599	-24.10	1.03
26	21:03:39	11.0	0.540	0.029	92	0.540	86.9	-24.096	-0.221	0.493	91.7	1.599	-24.10	1.03
27	21:03:39	11.5	0.564	0.031	96	0.565	86.9	-24.096	-0.231	0.516	95.8	1.599	-24.10	1.03
28	21:03:38	12.0	0.589	0.032	100	0.589	86.9	-24.096	-0.241	0.538	100.0	1.599	-24.10	1.03
29	21:03:38	12.5	0.613	0.033	104	0.614	86.9	-24.096	-0.251	0.561	104.2	1.599	-24.10	1.03
30	21:03:37	13.0	0.638	0.034	108	0.639	86.9	-24.096	-0.261	0.583	108.3	1.599	-24.10	1.03
31	21:03:37	13.5	0.662	0.036	111	0.663	86.9	-24.096	-0.271	0.605	110.8	1.576	-24.10	1.01
32	21:03:36	14.0	0.687	0.037	112	0.688	86.9	-24.096	-0.281	0.628	111.7	1.531	-24.10	0.97
33	21:03:36	14.5	0.711	0.038	112	0.712	86.9	-24.096	-0.291	0.650	112.5	1.489	-24.10	0.92
34	21:03:35	15.0	0.736	0.040	113	0.737	86.9	-24.096	-0.301	0.673	113.3	1.450	-24.10	0.88
35	21:03:35	15.5	0.760	0.041	114	0.761	86.9	-24.096	-0.311	0.695	114.2	1.414	-24.10	0.85
36	21:03:34	16.0	0.785	0.042	115	0.786	86.9	-24.096	-0.321	0.717	115.0	1.380	-24.10	0.81
37	21:03:34	16.5	0.809	0.044	116	0.810	86.9	-24.096	-0.331	0.740	115.8	1.347	-24.10	0.78
38	21:03:33	17.0	0.834	0.045	117	0.835	86.9	-24.096	-0.341	0.762	116.7	1.317	-24.10	0.75
39	21:03:33	17.5	0.858	0.046	117	0.860	86.9	-24.096	-0.351	0.785	117.5	1.289	-24.10	0.72
40	21:03:32	18.0	0.883	0.048	118	0.884	86.9	-23.447	-0.352	0.811	118.3	1.262	-22.97	-5.42
41	21:03:32	18.5	0.908	0.050	119	0.909	86.9	-21.411	-0.332	0.846	119.2	1.236	-19.16	-10.32
42	21:03:31	19.0	0.932	0.052	120	0.934	86.8	-18.656	-0.299	0.885	120.0	1.211	-16.76	-9.39
43	21:03:31	19.5	0.958	0.055	121	0.959	86.7	-15.942	-0.263	0.922	120.8	1.188	-14.40	-8.05
44	21:03:30	20.0	0.983	0.059	122	0.985	86.6	-13.265	-0.226	0.958	121.7	1.165	-12.07	-6.73

Figure 4.5 Spreadsheet used to calculate the bearing angles from aircraft 1 to aircraft 2.

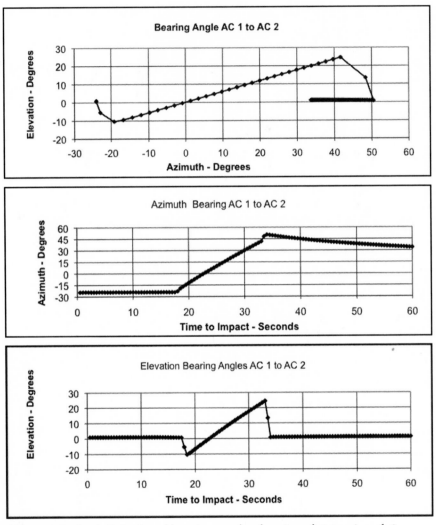

Figure 4.5a (top) Calculated bearing angles for aircraft 1 to aircraft 2, azimuth vs. elevation.

Figure 4.5b (middle) Calculated bearing angles for aircraft 1 to aircraft 2, azimuth vs. time to impact.

Figure 4.5c (bottom) Calculated bearing angles for aircraft 1 to aircraft 2, elevation vs. time to impact.

	A	B	C	D	E	F	G	H	I	J	K	L	M	N
1	AC 2 Bearing Angles to AC 1													
2														
3	Time	T	dX	dY	dZ	R(x,y)	AZ0	AZ1	dX	dY	dZ	EL1	AZ2	EL2
4	21:03:50	0												
5	21:03:50	0.5	-0.02	0.00	-4	0.02	-93.10	40.46	0.02	0.02	-4	-1.60	40.46	2.21
6	21:03:49	1.0	-0.05	0.00	-8	0.05	-93.10	40.46	0.03	0.04	-8	-1.60	40.46	2.21
7	21:03:49	1.5	-0.07	0.00	-12	0.07	-93.10	40.46	0.05	0.06	-12	-1.60	40.46	2.21
8	21:03:48	2.0	-0.10	-0.01	-17	0.10	-93.10	40.46	0.06	0.07	-17	-1.60	40.46	2.21
9	21:03:48	2.5	-0.12	-0.01	-21	0.12	-93.10	40.46	0.08	0.09	-21	-1.60	40.46	2.21
10	21:03:47	3.0	-0.15	-0.01	-25	0.15	-93.10	40.46	0.10	0.11	-25	-1.60	40.46	2.21
11	21:03:47	3.5	-0.17	-0.01	-29	0.17	-93.10	40.46	0.11	0.13	-29	-1.60	40.46	2.21
12	21:03:46	4.0	-0.20	-0.01	-33	0.20	-93.10	40.46	0.13	0.15	-33	-1.60	40.46	2.21
13	21:03:46	4.5	-0.22	-0.01	-37	0.22	-93.10	40.46	0.14	0.17	-37	-1.60	40.46	2.21
14	21:03:45	5.0	-0.25	-0.01	-42	0.25	-93.10	40.46	0.16	0.19	-42	-1.60	40.46	2.21
15	21:03:45	5.5	-0.27	-0.01	-46	0.27	-93.10	40.46	0.18	0.21	-46	-1.60	40.46	2.21
16	21:03:44	6.0	-0.29	-0.02	-50	0.29	-93.10	40.46	0.19	0.22	-50	-1.60	40.46	2.21
17	21:03:44	6.5	-0.32	-0.02	-54	0.32	-93.10	40.46	0.21	0.24	-54	-1.60	40.46	2.21
18	21:03:43	7.0	-0.34	-0.02	-58	0.34	-93.10	40.46	0.22	0.26	-58	-1.60	40.46	2.21
19	21:03:43	7.5	-0.37	-0.02	-62	0.37	-93.10	40.46	0.24	0.28	-62	-1.60	40.46	2.21
20	21:03:42	8.0	-0.39	-0.02	-67	0.39	-93.10	40.46	0.26	0.30	-67	-1.60	40.46	2.21
21	21:03:42	8.5	-0.42	-0.02	-71	0.42	-93.10	40.46	0.27	0.32	-71	-1.60	40.46	2.21
22	21:03:41	9.0	-0.44	-0.02	-75	0.44	-93.10	40.46	0.29	0.34	-75	-1.60	40.46	2.21
23	21:03:41	9.5	-0.47	-0.03	-79	0.47	-93.10	40.46	0.30	0.36	-79	-1.60	40.46	2.21
24	21:03:40	10.0	-0.49	-0.03	-83	0.49	-93.10	40.46	0.32	0.37	-83	-1.60	40.46	2.21
25	21:03:40	10.5	-0.52	-0.03	-87	0.52	-93.10	40.46	0.33	0.39	-87	-1.60	40.46	2.21
26	21:03:39	11.0	-0.54	-0.03	-92	0.54	-93.10	40.46	0.35	0.41	-92	-1.60	40.46	2.21
27	21:03:39	11.5	-0.56	-0.03	-96	0.56	-93.10	40.46	0.37	0.43	-96	-1.60	40.46	2.21
28	21:03:38	12.0	-0.59	-0.03	-100	0.59	-93.10	40.46	0.38	0.45	-100	-1.60	40.46	2.21
29	21:03:38	12.5	-0.61	-0.03	-104	0.61	-93.10	40.46	0.40	0.47	-104	-1.60	40.46	2.21
30	21:03:37	13.0	-0.64	-0.03	-108	0.64	-93.10	40.46	0.41	0.49	-108	-1.60	40.46	2.21
31	21:03:37	13.5	-0.66	-0.04	-111	0.66	-93.10	40.46	0.43	0.50	-111	-1.58	40.46	2.19
32	21:03:36	14.0	-0.69	-0.04	-112	0.69	-93.10	40.46	0.45	0.52	-112	-1.53	40.46	-0.34
33	21:03:36	14.5	-0.71	-0.04	-112	0.71	-93.10	40.46	0.46	0.54	-112	-1.49	40.46	-0.38
34	21:03:35	15.0	-0.74	-0.04	-113	0.74	-93.10	40.46	0.48	0.56	-113	-1.45	40.46	-0.42
35	21:03:35	15.5	-0.76	-0.04	-114	0.76	-93.10	40.46	0.49	0.58	-114	-1.41	40.46	-0.46
36	21:03:34	16.0	-0.78	-0.04	-115	0.79	-93.10	40.46	0.51	0.60	-115	-1.38	40.46	-0.49
37	21:03:34	16.5	-0.81	-0.04	-116	0.81	-93.10	40.46	0.53	0.62	-116	-1.35	40.46	-0.53
38	21:03:33	17.0	-0.83	-0.05	-117	0.84	-93.10	40.46	0.54	0.64	-117	-1.32	40.46	-0.56
39	21:03:33	17.5	-0.86	-0.05	-117	0.86	-93.10	40.46	0.56	0.65	-117	-1.29	40.46	-0.58
40	21:03:32	18.0	-0.88	-0.05	-118	0.88	-93.10	40.46	0.57	0.67	-118	-1.26	40.46	-0.61
41	21:03:32	18.5	-0.91	-0.05	-119	0.91	-93.13	40.43	0.59	0.69	-119	-1.24	40.43	-0.64
42	21:03:31	19.0	-0.93	-0.05	-120	0.93	-93.19	40.37	0.60	0.71	-120	-1.21	40.37	-0.66
43	21:03:31	19.5	-0.96	-0.06	-121	0.96	-93.29	40.27	0.62	0.73	-121	-1.19	40.27	-0.68
44	21:03:30	20.0	-0.98	-0.06	-122	0.98	-93.43	40.13	0.63	0.75	-122	-1.17	40.13	-0.71

Figure 4.6 *Spreadsheet used to calculate the bearing angles from aircraft 2 to aircraft 1.*

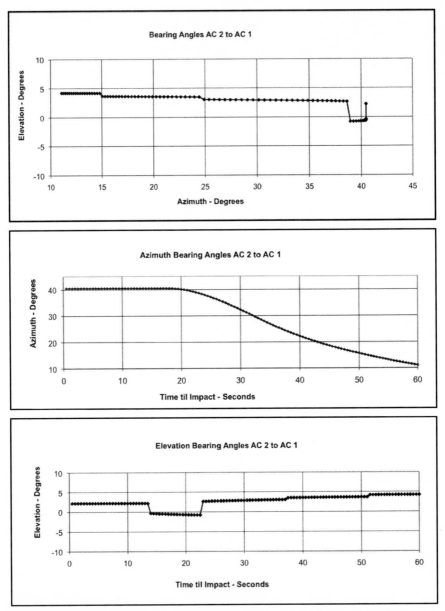

Figure 4.6a (top) Calculated bearing angles for aircraft 2 to aircraft 1, azimuth vs. elevation.

Figure 4.6b (middle) Calculated bearing angles for aircraft 2 to aircraft 1, azimuth vs. time to impact.

Figure 4.6c (bottom) Calculated bearing angles for aircraft 2 to aircraft 1, elevation vs. time to impact.

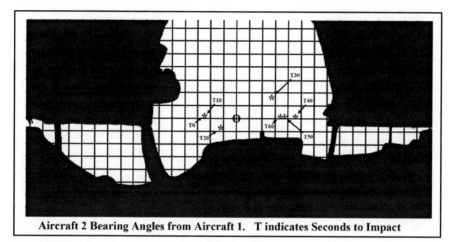

Aircraft 2 Bearing Angles from Aircraft 1. T indicates Seconds to Impact

Figure 4.7 Cockpit field of view with aircraft 1 bearing angles to aircraft 2 with T indicating time to impact in seconds.

Figure 4.6 is a similar worksheet, and Figure 4.6a, Figure 4.6b, and Figure 4.6c, are similar graphs, for bearing angles from Aircraft 2 to Aircraft 1.

The bearing angle information shows where the opposing aircraft would have appeared within the cockpit field of view of each aircraft. Appropriate cockpit field of view information for some aircraft types have been documented in Federal Aviation Administration studies.[1] This research effort involved the use of a binocular camera system mounted at pilot eye height in a large number of commercial and private aircraft types. The binocular aspect of this documentation can be of importance if the bearing angle calculations place the target aircraft in the vicinity of cockpit field of view limitations, such as window posts. Our eyes are separated by something on the order of 2.5 inches, which is the distance chosen for separation of the two lenses in the binocular camera system. The importance of the binocular view is that a target blocked from the view of one eye may be available for viewing by the other eye. It is also important to recognize that pilots need to move their heads to see around cockpit field of view restraints. Figure 4.7 is an example of a monocular cockpit field of view. The bearing angle data generated in the illustrative example has been added to the cockpit field of view to demonstrate the location of the line of sight to the target aircraft at selected times before impact. The zero azimuth and elevation position is marked with the "O." The horizontal and vertical lines define the azimuth and elevation bearing angles at 10 degree intervals.

If cockpit field of view data is not available for the aircraft type involved, documentation can be accomplished photographically. When photographs are taken with the aircraft parked on the ground, it is important to take note of the pitch attitude of the aircraft, and document the pitch by taking an external side view photo. This takes on particular importance if the bearing angle calculations place the target aircraft in close proximity to the upper or lower boundary of the cockpit field of view. It is also important to establish both a vertical and a horizontal reference for the photographs. For the vertical reference, this can be done by using a "bubble level" on the camera or by noting a distant reference point, as for example the horizon in a flat scene. The horizontal reference can be established by marking or noting a specific item on the instrument panel that is located directly ahead of the camera lens. The angular distance between points in the images can be calculated knowing the focal length of the lens and the dimensions of the camera image detector array.

It is sometimes useful to display the results of the flight path calculations in the form of a computer animation. This can be accomplished using animation software such as 3D Studios. Three-dimensional models are available for many aircraft make and models. The flight path data can be used to position and orient the models. A "software camera" can be placed in each of the aircraft at the pilot's eye position. Terrain profile data detailing the ground features can be purchased and coupled with satellite photography of the terrain in that region. In the animation software the satellite photos can be projected onto the terrain. The

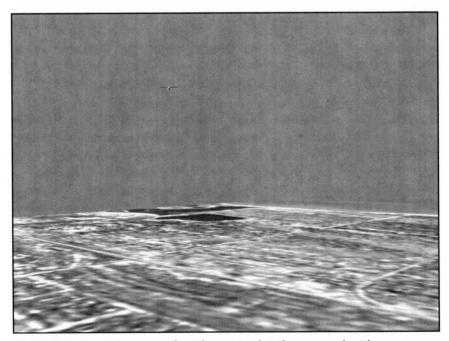

Figure 4.8 *View of an aircraft with terrain detail generated with computer animation software.*

software allows for placement of the sun at the proper location for a specified location and time of day. Figure 4.8 is an example of a single frame from such a simulation.

The animation can be used to demonstrate visual search for the pilot by aiming the animation camera at selected azimuth and elevation bearing angles for a period of time consistent with a plausible search pattern, as for example 1 second.

4.3 Capabilities and Limitations of Visual Search

Generally the goal associated with all of the activities just described is to be able to deal with the question as to whether either or both of the pilots involved should have been able to "see and avoid" the collision. The analysis may show that the pilot or pilots had an unobstructed view of the other aircraft and that, had they looked in that direction at the proper time, they would have been able to see the other aircraft. Caution must be exercised in finding the pilot responsible for the collision on that basis, without taking into consideration the details associated with the performance of an appropriate visual search. Published advice as to procedure for performing a proper scan for other aircraft suggests that:

> Scanning the sky for other aircraft is a key factor in collision avoidance. It should be used continuously by the pilot or copilot (or right seat passenger) to cover all areas of the sky visible from the cockpit.[2]

It is also stated that:

> While the eyes can observe an approximate 200 degree arc of the horizon at one glance, only a very small center area called the central fovea, in the rear of the eye, has the ability to send clear, sharply focused messages to the brain.[2]

And also,

> Because the eyes can focus only on this narrow viewing area effective scanning is accomplished with a series of short, regularly spaced eye movements that bring successive areas of the sky into the central visual field. Each movement should not exceed 10 degrees, and each area should be observed for at least 1 second to enable detection.[2]

That same reference also suggests that the pilot should spend no more than 20 percent of the time in internal cockpit activity leaving 80 percent of the time available for external visual search. Assuming these suggested criteria are used by the pilot, a search conducted from 90 degrees left to 90 degrees right at 10 degree azimuth intervals would involve 19 eye movements, each taking 1 second, resulting in a total time period of 19 seconds for a complete scan. If the proportion of time spent with eyes in the cockpit was 20 percent, then the total time between external scans would be approximately 24 seconds. These are important considerations and deserve to be considered in some detail in the sections that follow.

4.4 Factors Influencing Visual Search Strategy

Ideally, the strategy for visual search should be based upon knowledge as to the relative importance of exploring various regions within the cockpit field of view. In an attempt to provide insight into this matter, several numerical examples will be presented. For the first example, assume that the two aircraft involved are travelling at the same speed. Figure 4.9 is a plan view with Aircraft 1 located at the point of the asterisk located between the two arrows.

The point of impact is shown at the center of the circle. Aircraft 2 is located at any position on the circle. Figure 4.10 is a graph of the horizontal and vertical bearing angles that would occur assuming both aircraft are traveling at 120 knots with a climb rate differential between the two aircraft of 2000 feet per minute. A rough approximation of the "Cockpit Field of View" is shown to draw attention to the fact that there are bearing angles outside of the typical field of view available to the pilot. The discontinuity at an Azimuth of 0 degrees, reflects the fact that Aircraft 2 could be directly above or below Aircraft 1 so that the line of sight is directly up or directly down. It should be noted that at any location on the circle, Aircraft 2 is the same time away from impact, but that the distance between the two aircraft decreases with increasing bearing angle. At 0 degrees bearing angle the view of the other aircraft is a nose-on cross-section. As the bearing angle increases the perspective moves to a side view. Both of these changes make Aircraft 2 more easily visible. This effect will be discussed in more detail below.

Figure 4.11 is a plan view similar to Figure 4.9 but with Aircraft 1 airspeed half of that of Aircraft 2. The horizontal bearing angle from Aircraft 1 to Aircraft 2 is now anywhere from 0 to 360 degrees. Figure 4.12 is a graph of the limits of the Azimuth and Elevation bearing angles from Aircraft 1 to Aircraft 2 assuming an airspeed for Aircraft 1 of 120 knots, an airspeed for Aircraft 2 of 240 knots, and a climb rate differential of +/- 2000 feet per minute. From Aircraft 1 to Aircraft 2, cockpit field of view limitations can prevent visibility of the other aircraft for many possible azimuth bearing angles.

Figure 4.13 is the plan view under the reverse condition such that Aircraft 1 has twice the airspeed of Aircraft 2. The double-arrow is to note that for any

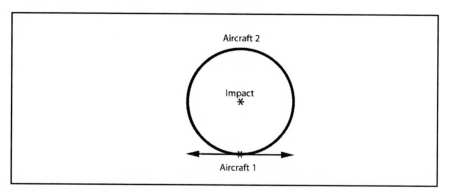

Figure 4.9 *Plan view sketch showing all bearing angles from aircraft 1 to aircraft 2 at which there could be a collision threat, assuming both aircraft have identical speed.*

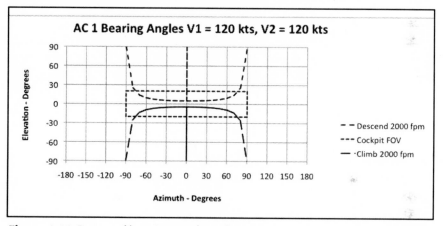

Figure 4.10 *Range of bearing angles, elevation vs. azimuth, where collision threat aircraft could be located, assuming both aircraft have identical speed.*

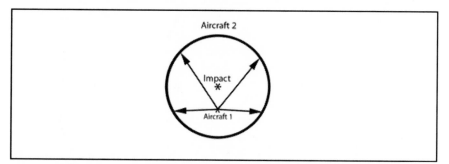

Figure 4.11 *Bearing angles from aircraft 1 to aircraft 2 at which there could be a collision threat, assuming aircraft 2 has twice the speed of aircraft 1.*

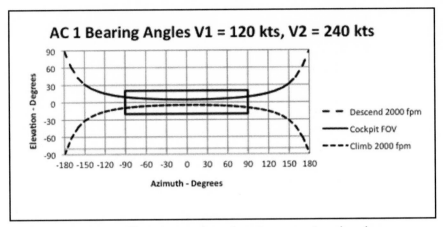

Figure 4.12 *Range of bearing angles, elevation vs. azimuth, where collision threat aircraft could be located, assuming aircraft 2 has twice the speed of aircraft 1.*

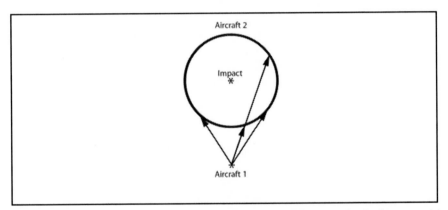

Figure 4.13 *Bearing angles from aircraft 1 to aircraft 2 at which there could be a collision threat, assuming aircraft 2 has half the speed of aircraft 1.*

given azimuth bearing angle there will be two possible locations for Aircraft 2: one closer than the other but with a greater elevation angle. Figure 4.14 is the graph of the limits of azimuth and elevation bearing angles of Aircraft 2 from the cockpit of Aircraft 1. As before, it is assumed that there is a climb rate differential of 2000 feet per minute. Under these conditions the line of sight of Aircraft 2 from the cockpit of Aircraft 1 will be well within the cockpit field of view. While it is true that faster aircraft will generally have greater cross-sections than the slower aircraft, making their visual detection less difficult, it is likely that collision avoidance due to "see and avoid" will depend upon the actions of the faster

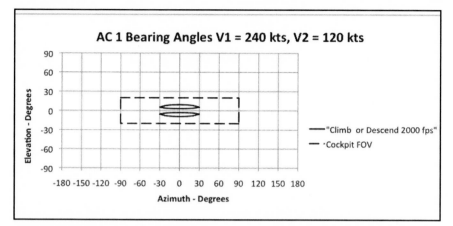

Figure 4.14 *Bearing angles, elevation vs. azimuth, where collision threat aircraft could be located, assuming aircraft 2 has half the speed of aircraft 1.*

aircraft due to the smaller bounds of azimuth at which the slower aircraft will appear.

As previously discussed, if the referenced Aeronautical Information Manual "search rules" are utilized, there would be 24 seconds between scans.[2] Using the arbitrarily suggested speeds used in the previous collision encounter examples, at 360 knots closing speed, the range would decrease by 0.1 nautical miles per second, or a total of a little over 2 nautical miles in the time between scans. If the collision threat was not detected at 2 nautical miles, it may not be detected prior to collision. How difficult is it to accomplish visual detection at 2 nautical miles?

Obviously, there are many factors that alter aircraft visibility. This includes the sun position, the aircraft paint scheme, and the reflectance and complexity of the background against which the aircraft is viewed. In an attempt to aid in visualizing the search task involved, Figure 4.15 was generated. This sequence of images of a Cessna 172, when viewed at the proper distance, shows the angular size and level of detail that is visible at distances from 500 feet to 2 nautical miles. The viewing distance should be six times the width of the arrow at the bottom of Figure 4.15. That viewing distance is therefore dependent on the size of the final printing of Figure 4.15. When viewed at that distance, the overall width of the arrow is approximately 10 degrees. If we fixate on the border of Figure 4.15, which would be 5 degrees away from the aircraft image, we can observe that the image of the aircraft at 2 nautical miles is nearly invisible. When we perform such a test, we do so being aware that the aircraft image is indeed present. To a pilot who is unaware of the presence of an aircraft at that location, it is doubtful that

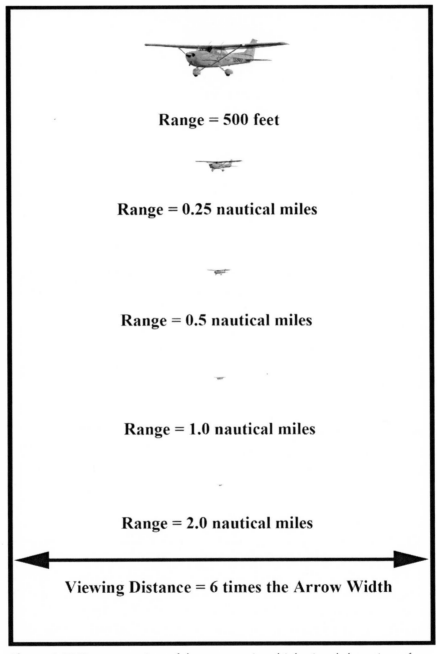

Figure 4.15 *Demonstration of the manner in which visual detection of an aircraft decreases with viewing distance and peripheral target location.*

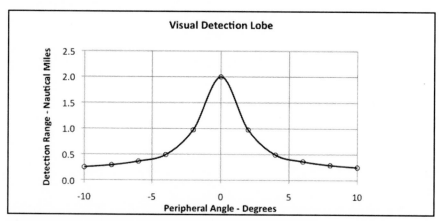

Figure 4.15a *A visual detection lobe showing how detection range decreases with increase in peripheral angle of viewing.*

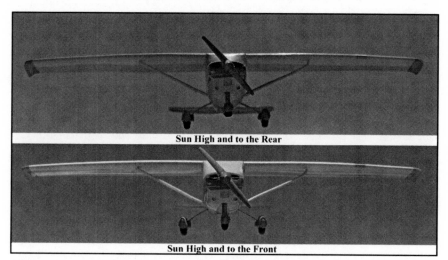

Figure 4.16 *Two photographs of a Cessna 150 model, one with the sun high and to the rear of the aircraft, and the second with the sun high and to the front.*

detection of the aircraft would occur. This is consistent with the Federal Aviation Administration, that in the visual search, "eye movement should not exceed 10 degrees, and each area should be observed for at least 1 second to enable detection."[2] If we fixate at a distance of 10 degrees from the image, which is twice the distance from the aircraft image to the border, you can see that the perception of the aircraft at 2 nautical miles has pretty much disappeared.

Figure 1.4, and the numerical data involved, shows the relative contrast thresholds as a function of where the target appears in the peripheral field of view. For targets with small angular size, the product of contrast and the square of the angular subtense determine visibility. So for a target located in the periphery, the given increase in contrast threshold can be offset by a decrease in the target range, specifically a decrease in range proportional to the square root of the contrast threshold increase. Using this data we can construct a visual detection lobe, which shows the detection range as a function of the peripheral location of the target. Figure 4.15a is an example of such a visual detection lobe, assuming that the target is detectable at 2 nautical miles when viewed in the center of the central fovea.

Hopefully, these examples will aid in understanding the limitations associated with visual search. The images of Figure 4.15 are for an aircraft viewed against a uniform sky background. Sun position is an important variable affecting aircraft detectability. Figure 4.16 includes two images of a Cessna 150, one with the sun high and to the front of the aircraft and the second with the sun high and to the rear of the of the aircraft. On a clear day, an aircraft viewed with the sun to the rear of the aircraft will generally have much of the aircraft surfaces darker than the sky background, that is, negative contrast.

Detection of anything in the sky, including a reduced resolution "blob," is a matter of interest. The background against which the aircraft is sighted is of great importance in determining its detectability. For example a complex cloud pattern can have a large influence on the contrast of the aircraft and its detectability. It is very unlikely that the images of Figure 4.15, viewed against a complex terrain background, would be visually detected.

Two aircraft travelling at constant speed on a collision course will result in "constancy of bearing" so that motion will not be a helpful factor in generating peripheral detection. However, if a terrain background is at a substantially greater distance than the threat aircraft, there may be movement of the aircraft with respect to the terrain background, which will increase the probability of visual detection, both foveally and peripherally.

4.5 Visual Search Strategy

The plan for performing visual search should be based upon maximizing the probability that important information will be obtained. Hopefully the examples that have been shown make it clear that the optimum strategy in terms of the distribution of search time within the cockpit field of view depends upon the bearing angle of the threat aircraft and upon the velocity of each aircraft involved. Also, as the bearing angle of the threat aircraft is increased, the closing velocity is reduced, and the view of the threat aircraft will include more of a side view having a larger cross sectional area. As a result, the optimum search pattern should dictate spending less time in searching the higher bearing angles. As previously stated, if a search is conducted from 90 degrees left to 90 degrees right with 10 degree eye movements, there would be 19 eye movements, each taking 1 second resulting in a total time period of 19 seconds for a complete scan. If the proportion of time spent with eyes in the cockpit were 20 percent, then the total time between external scans would be approximately 24 seconds. If, for example, the closure speed is 360 knots (0.1 nautical miles per second), the aircraft will have closed by 2.4 nautical miles since the last scan. An Advisory Circular published by the FAA has an appendix titled, *A Radar for All Seasons*, which deals with numerical aspects of "see and avoid."[3] A chart is included that lists the timing of the series of events that take place between "see" and "avoid." According to this chart they are:

See object	0.1 seconds
Recognize a/c	1.0 seconds
Become aware of collision course	5.0 seconds
Decision to turn left or right	4.0 seconds
Muscular reaction time	0.4 seconds
Aircraft lag time	2.0 seconds
Total	**12.5 seconds**

If these numbers are valid, then with a 24-second time period since the last scan, visual detection needs to occur 36.5 seconds before impact in order to insure that there is time to achieve a successful evasive movement. For a closing speed of 360 knots this means the threat aircraft must be visible at a distance of 3.65 nautical miles. The probability that the visual search will involve a fixation placing the aircraft image directly on the central fovea is very small. In other words, this will most likely have to be detection at 3.65 nautical miles with peripheral vision. Figure 4.15 demonstrates that this may very well be an unlikely event.

There is no doubt that highly experienced professional pilots may develop insight into the probability of encountering various types of aircraft as a function of the specifics of their current situation and they may modify their search procedure accordingly. For example, an airline pilot, flying a flight path directed by Air Traffic Control, may expect that an unannounced encounter is more likely to happen with a smaller, lower speed aircraft that is not in communication with Air Traffic Control. This being the case, the bearing angle of such an aircraft will be nearly straight ahead so that more time should be spent in the forward directions than off to the side. As in the case of gambling, playing according to the odds does not mean that you will always win, because you may very well encounter unexpected circumstances.

Obviously, being advised as to the presence and bearing angle of another aircraft that is a possible collision threat is of dramatic importance. Being provided a "clock" type-bearing angle reduces the 180-degree search field to 30 degrees, greatly enhancing the success of a visual search. And even in cases where visual detection does not take place, Air Traffic Control may provide instructions for flight path modifications that will eliminate the collision threat.

4.6 Collision Avoidance

The FAA publication, *Midair Collision Avoidance, Your Role in Collision Avoidance*, offers the following advice:

Recent studies of midair collisions involving aircraft by the National Transportation Safety Board (NTSB) determined that:

- Most of the aircraft involved in collisions are engaged in recreational flying, not on any type of flight plan.
- Most midair collisions occur in VFR weather conditions during weekend daylight hours.
- The vast majority of accidents occurred at or near uncontrolled airports and at altitudes below 1000 feet.
- Pilots of all experience levels were involved in midair collisions, from pilots on their first solo flight, to 20,000-hour veterans.
- Flight instructors were on board the aircraft 37 percent of the accidents in the study.
- Most collisions occur in daylight with visibility greater than 3 miles.

Here's how *you* can contribute to professional flying and reduce the odds of becoming involved in a midair collision.

1. Practice the "see and avoid" concept at all times regardless of whether the operation is conducted under Instrument (IFR) or Visual (VFR) Flight Rules.
2. Under IFR control, don't always count on ATC to keep you away from other aircraft. They're human, and can make mistakes.
3. Understand the limitations of your eyes and use proper visual scanning techniques. Remember, if another aircraft appears to have no

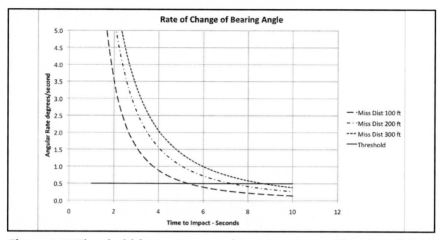

Figure 4.17 *Threshold for sensing angular movement as a function of time to impact for two aircraft with 90 degree heading difference with both aircraft traveling at a speed of 120 knots.*

relative motion, but is increasing in size, it is likely to be on a collision course with you.

4.   Execute appropriate clearing procedures before all climbs, descents, turns, training maneuvers or acrobatics.

5.   Be aware of the type airspace in which you intend to operate in and comply with the applicable rules.

6.   Adhere to the necessary communications requirements.

7.   Traffic advisories should be requested and used when available to assist the pilot's own visual scanning—advisories in no way lessen the pilot's obligation to see and avoid.

8.   If not practical to initiate radio contact for traffic information, at least monitor the appropriate frequency.

9.   Make frequent position reports along your route and *AT UNCONTROLLED AIRPORTS BROADCAST YOUR POSITION AND INTENTIONS ON COMMON TRAFFIC ADVISORY FREQUENCY (CTAF)*.

10. Make your aircraft as visible as possible—turn on exterior lights below 10,000 MSL and landing lights when operating within 10 miles of any airport, in conditions of reduced visibility where any bird activity is expected or under special VFR clearance.

11. If the aircraft is equipped with a transponder, turn it on and adjust it to reply on both Mode 3/A and Mode C (if installed). Transponders substantially increase the capability of radar to see all aircraft and

the MODE C feature enables the controller to quickly determine where potential traffic conflicts exist. Even VFR pilot who are not in contact with ATC will be afforded greater protection from IFR aircraft receiving traffic advisories.[3]

Visual acquisition of an aircraft is just the beginning of the process. Detection must be followed by an evaluation of the extent to which the aircraft does truly represent a potential for collision, and, if that evaluation is positive, the formulation of a plan for an appropriate evasive maneuver. Some situations are obvious. For example, if the aircraft that has been sighted is located to the right and has a heading to the right then it is not a collision threat. On the other hand if the aircraft is located to your right with a heading to your left then it is clear that the aircraft may be expected at some point to cross your flight path. The evaluation must also include the relative speed and altitude of the two aircraft.

The primary visual cue for evaluating a potential collision encounter is sensing angular movement. If an aircraft appears to be moving to the left or right, then it will pass to the left or right of the sighting aircraft. Constancy of bearing is the criterion for a collision. Experiments have shown that the visual threshold

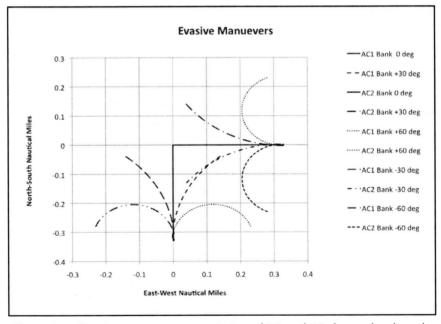

Figure 4.18 *Evasive maneuvers consisting of 30 and 60 degree bank and turns in either direction for two aircraft with 90 degree heading difference with both aircraft traveling at a speed of 120 knots.*

for being able to detect angular motion is on the order of 0.3 degrees per second. In a cockpit environment it is likely that the threshold is more like 0.5 degrees per second. This means that, if an aircraft is sighted that does not "appear" to be moving in either azimuth or elevation, its angular movement, if any, is below that threshold. For example, assume that we have two aircraft, each at a velocity of 120 knots, on headings separated by 90 degrees. If they are truly on a collision course then the azimuth and elevation angles will not appear to change with time. However, because of the threshold limitation associated with sensing the change in angle, they may actually be on a "near miss course." Figure 4.17 illustrates the effect of this angular movement threshold. It shows the rate of change of azimuth bearing angle as a function of time before impact from 0 to 10 seconds, for situations involving miss distances of 100, 200, and 300 feet. The threshold for sensing closure is shown by the horizontal line located at 0.5 degrees per second. The intersection of each of the three curves with that threshold line shows the time before impact at which the movement in azimuth will become perceptible. For example, if there is actually a miss distance of 300 feet, the movement in azimuth will not become noticeable until about 8 seconds before impact. This opens up the possibility that a near miss may turn into a collision because of a maneuver based upon a sighting, which appeared to have constancy of bearing. The author has encountered midair collisions in which investigators have stated that the pilot attempted to maneuver to avoid the collision but it was "too late." Factually, in some cases, the maneuver turned a near miss into a collision. This is not to say that the pilots are necessarily at fault in these accidents; it simply points out the limitations that angular movement thresholds impose.

The previously referenced document suggests that, when a potential collision threat is sighted, 4 seconds be used to make the "decision to turn left or right." If there is angular movement of the threat aircraft, this indicates a near miss rather than a collision and the response should be to make a turn in the direction opposite that of the angular movement so as to increase the miss distance. If no angular movement is sensed, the decision as to the proper maneuver is more complicated. Figure 4.18 is a set of calculations showing two aircraft on a collision course. The calculation assumes an airspeed of 120 knots for both aircraft. Aircraft 1 is headed due north and Aircraft 2 is headed due west with the point of impact at 0,0 on the graph. The calculations show the path of the two aircraft for the last 10 seconds of flight. The graph shows the flight paths for each aircraft if, at the 10 second point, they each made a bank and turn to the left or to the right and with bank angles of 30 degrees and 60 degrees. A serious problem for the pilots is that they do not know what evasive action, if any, will be taken by the other aircraft. If possible, the selected evasive action should be such that it will be successful no matter what evasive action is taken by the other aircraft. Keeping that objective in mind we can evaluate each of the four evasive maneuvers shown from the perspective of Aircraft 1. In making such an evaluation we must keep in mind that even though no angular movement was sensed, the two aircraft may have been on a near-miss encounter and the desired response would be a maneuver that would result in a wide separation. The 60 degree bank and turn to the right would not be a successful maneuver if Aircraft 2 made a 60 degree bank and turn to the left. The 30 degree bank and turn to the right would not be a successful maneuver if Aircraft 2 made a 30 degree bank and turn to the left. If Aircraft 1 made a 30 degree bank and turn to the left this would not be a successful maneuver if Aircraft 2 took no evasive action because it would cause Aircraft 1 to cross over the projected flight path of Aircraft 2 at a time later than the no-action collision. Of the four maneuvers shown in this example, the only one shown for Aircraft 1 that would be successful, regardless of the evasive action of Aircraft 2, is the 60 degree bank and turn to the left.

It would be very helpful if there was a "rule of the road" for evasive action in a potential collision encounter; one that is so simple and well-known that pilots would apply it as a reflex action. The hope would be that visual sighting of the collision threat aircraft takes place at a time before impact sufficient to allow visualizing the flight path of the threat aircraft and taking action to see that the two flight paths do not intersect. The decisions become more difficult when the visual acquisition takes place with little time for action. As previously stated, when angular movement of the collision threat aircraft is sensed, this indicates a near miss and any maneuver should be to turn in a direction opposite to the sensed movement in order to increase the miss distance. When no angular movement is sensed the decision as to a course of action is much more complex. The decision is made more difficult by the fact that it is likely that this is a "first time" experience for the pilots involved. A computer simulated "collision avoidance game" would be a useful tool. It is also possible that one aircraft will take evasive action that negates the action taken by the other aircraft.

A possible maneuver that can be significant in the last few seconds before impact is discussed in a previous publication.[4] In sword fighting, the best way to block an opponents sword headed in your direction is to place your sword at right angles to the oncoming blade. This greatly increases the probability that the two swords will collide. Aircraft, like swords, have horizontal dimensions much greater than the vertical dimensions due to the wing structure. If two aircraft approach each other in a collision or near miss situation, each banked at a 45-degree angle, the two wing surfaces will be at a 90-degree angle, and the potential collision cross section is increased by a factor of as much as 3 to 1. Therefore if, immediately before impact, the bank angle can be altered to make the two wings parallel, this can result in a 3 to 1 decrease in the probability of collision.

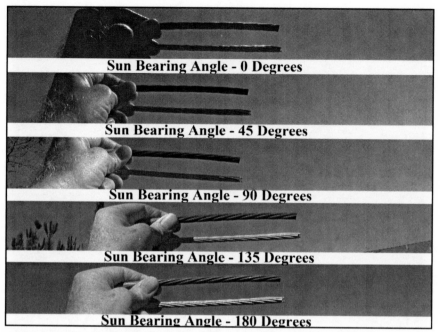

Figure 4.19 *Composite of five photographs showing new and aged static line samples viewed against sky backgrounds, each with a different sun-bearing angle.*

4.7 Aircraft Wire Strikes

The visibility questions generally associated with an aircraft wire strike are, 1) Should the pilot have been able to visually detect the power line at a distance sufficient to allow time to accomplish an evasive maneuver? and, 2) Would the presence of ball markers on the line have prevented the accident?

4.8 Visual Detection of Power Lines

There are a number of important factors that relate to the visibility of power lines. The physical size of the conductor and the distance to the conductor determine the angular size of the conductor as it is imaged on the retina of the eye. In the wire strike accidents the author has investigated, there have been "static lines" above the main conductors. The static lines were typically $^{3}/_{8}$ inches in diameter, and the main conductors approximately 1.5 inches. The reflectance of the conductors depends upon their composition and the length of time they have been in service. The luminance of the conductors depends upon the lighting geometry with the sun position and cloud conditions playing a major role. Figure 4.19 is a composite of five photos of two different samples of static line having

Figure 4.20 *Two photographs of a power line taken within a few seconds time during which the sun was initially behind a small cloud and then emerged from behind the cloud.*

substantially different reflectance. The photos were taken on a clear sunny day with each of the set taken with a different orientation with respect to the sun. It is important to note that with the Sun Bearing Angle of 180 degrees (direct sunlight on the conductors), both samples have a positive contrast, that is, luminance greater than the background, whereas with Sun Bearing Angles of 0, 45 and 90 degrees, both samples have a negative contrast, that is, luminance less than the background. This makes it clear that there will be a sun position with respect to the conductors that will result in a luminance match to the background, resulting in zero contrast.

The resolution of the human eye with 20/20 acuity is approximately 1 arc minute (1/60 degree). The $3/8$-inch line would subtend approximately 1 arc minute at a distance of 100 feet. It is important to recognize that the illumination of the static line is not uniform. The lower portion of the line receives the major

Figure 4.21 Photograph showing an overhead power line in which the lines are visible against the sky background at the top of the picture but are not visible when the background becomes a terrain background.

portion of its illumination from the ground than from the sky. On a clear sunny day, the illumination directly from sunlight may be as much as ten times the illumination from the entire sky. As can be seen from the photos, the illumination on the static line from the sun will depend upon the position of the sun with respect to the line of sight of an observer of the wire and will vary from the top to the bottom of the line. The importance of all of these factors is that at a distance of 100 feet, the perceived luminance (brightness) of the line will be the average of the luminance over the diameter of the line. Therefore, the observed luminance of the conductor will be dramatically influenced by the extent of the sunlight and the position of the sun in the sky. At distances beyond 100 feet, the limited resolution of the human eye will result in the fact that the perceived visual image will be an average of some percentage of the average conductor luminance and the luminance of the background. For example, at a distance of 200 feet the perceived luminance will be 50 percent of the average conductor luminance plus 50 percent of the background luminance. At a distance of 1000 feet, the perceived luminance will be 10 percent of the wire luminance and 90 percent of the background luminance. This factor results in a rapid decrease of apparent contrast of the conductors with respect to the background against which they are viewed.

A power line viewed against a uniform sky background can sometimes be viewed at distances well beyond the distance at which it is resolved by the human eye. This results from the fact that, if the initial contrast of the line is high, the eye can sense a lengthy continuity of the image of the conductor even though the contrast is substantially reduced due to being visually unresolved. However, if the line is viewed against a non-uniform terrain background, this continuity will be destroyed and the conductor will not be visible.

The importance of these various factors is that the visibility of conductors can be highly variable depending upon the exact position of the observer with respect to the conductor, the exact lighting conditions, and the nature and luminance of the background against which the conductor is being viewed. The author has visited a wire strike accident site where, from a ground position, the conductors were nearly invisible, but when the sun came out from behind a small cloud, the conductors became quite visible. Figure 4.20 shows two photos taken within seconds of each other: the top one with the sun behind a cloud and the bottom one with direct sunlight on the conductors. This presents a problem for those who investigate wire strikes, in that what is seen during a post-accident site visit may not be an accurate representation of the viewing conditions that existed for the parties involved in the accident. Extreme caution needs to be exercised to guard against the generation of invalid opinions based on these post-accident observations.

4.9 Conductors Viewed Against a Terrain Background

Wires unresolved by the human visual system may be seen at some distance due to the extensive horizontal continuity. Against a terrain background, this continuity is destroyed and the wires disappear. Figure 4.21 is a photograph taken from the ground while visiting the site of a wire strike. It demonstrates that in situations where the wires may be visible against a sky background, these same wires are not visible against a terrain background.

There is also a ball marker, which, in this black and white image duplication, is not readily visible against the terrain background. In the color version of this image, the red marker has considerably higher visibility.

4.10 Ball Markers

The balls placed on static lines produce a dramatic difference in the ability to visually detect the presence of a power line. For example, a 24-inch diameter ball is visually resolvable at a distance of 6,875 feet. At the much shorter distances that are critical in an aircraft/wire encounter, the balls are well resolved. When you observe the balls you can see the difference in illumination of the top, bottom, left and right, as contrasted with simply seeing an average over the diameter of a $^3/_8$-inch wire. A common practice of alternating colors of the ball markers along the line, for example red, white, and orange, makes it extremely unlikely that the background against which the balls are viewed will be a color and luminance match to each differently colored ball. The net result is that, under favorable sunlight conditions, ball markers placed on a power line dramatically enhance the visibility of the line and show precisely the location of the small diameter static line. When the sun illumination is to the rear of the ball, the color of the ball will become much less apparent and the marker may become less visible against a terrain background.

4.11 Tower Detection

Pilots are taught that the sighting of poles or towers, where they are not obscured, is an important method of sensing the presence of a power line. The accuracy with which conductor elevation can be sensed from tower elevation depends upon the location of the observer with respect to the tower. It is certainly true that, if a pilot can see adjacent towers and maintains a reasonable distance above both towers as he travels a path between the towers, he will not encounter the conductors. A serious complication is introduced when the two adjacent towers are at significantly different terrain elevations. Under these conditions, where the towers are visible but the conductors are not, a pilot, unable to see the conductors, must either maintain a flight path above the highest tower or make a judgment about the mid-span height of the wire span above ground level. This leads to the possibility that the pilot may make incorrect conductor height estimates, which are based on false impressions, generated by his view of the scene. Obviously, ball markers eliminate the necessity of making such judgments as they clearly show the true location of the static line.

4.12 Line Marking Criteria

Clearly, not every power line needs to have ball markers. The decision as to when lines need to be marked is of great importance and involves the saving of human life. This fact led to a group action in California to attempt to aid in formulating criteria for making these decisions. Below are a couple of paragraphs from a document that they produced under the name, *Flight Safety Institute.*[5] Their activities may not have any legal significance, but they demonstrate the thinking of a diverse group of interested and knowledgeable parties. The following is copied from their report:

> Early in 1992, the Helicopter Association International (HAI), with the cooperation of the major utility companies in California, convened the Wire-Strike Prevention Task Force. This group consisted of senior representatives from helicopter companies, public service agencies (CHP, CDF, Sheriff's Departments, and so on), government agencies (F.A.A. Cal Trans), aviation associations (AOPA, HAI, and so on), military services, utility companies and other interested parties.

The Task Force's principal mandate was to develop a procedure for assessing potential wire-strike risks at field sites. After considering extensive factual data on airplane and helicopter wire-strike accidents, the comments of pilots, aircraft owners, government safety specialists and utility company engineers, and discussing the merits and limitations of various proposals, the Task Force unanimously agreed on a proposed "Wire-Strike Risk Assessment Methodology."

Field utilization of the "risk assessment methodology" requires the Evaluator to visit the site and make a determination in two critical areas:

1.   Visibility of the wires, and
2.   Likelihood of aircraft in the area at the wire's altitude.

In their evaluation technique, each of these two questions is scored on a 0 to 10 level and then a criterion for marking is based on the combination of these two separate scores. In terms of the wire visibility they denoted a 0 as meaning "Unmistakable" and a 10 as being "Virtually Impossible to See." For the likelihood of aircraft in the area at wire's altitude, they denoted a 0 as being "Remote" and a 10 as "Frequent." To demonstrate the relative weight that they placed on these two areas, if the visibility of the wires scored a 9 out of 10 or higher (Virtually Impossible to See) and the likelihood of aircraft scored a 1 out of 10 (Remote Likelihood of Aircraft in the Area), the conclusion was that the wires should be marked.

4.13 Pilot Responsibilities

Pilots have an obligation to use all of their resources to make themselves familiar with power lines in the regions in which they intend to fly at low levels. This would include studying charts that show power line locations. They also have an obligation, prior to descending to a lower altitude, to fly at altitudes well above the power lines to attempt to observe towers or poles allowing them to determine the location and direction of the transmission line. Humans perform visual search, pointing our eyes in different directions, based on a mental priority list as to what is deemed to be of importance in the present environment. When conducting flights in a region known to have power lines, avoidance of the wires must remain at the top of that priority list. If the pilot shifts her attention and priority toward some other goal associated with the flight, then the capability for sensing critical information about the power line will be dramatically reduced and this can lead to a wire strike accident. But even when a pilot's attention is misdirected, the presence of high conspicuity ball markers on the line offers the best possible strategy for bringing the pilot's attention back to the presence of the power line.

In attempting to evaluate the pilot's responsibility for a wire strike, it is important to take into consideration the specifics of the incident. This would include the inherent limitations with respect to the sighting of the conductors and the possibility of inaccurate visual perceptions of conductor location based on the sighting of adjacent towers located at substantially different terrain elevations.

4.14 Wire Strike Summary

In the evaluation of the visibility issues involved in a wire strike, it is essential that any observations be made under the conditions that existed for the pilot of the aircraft involved. This requires viewing from an accurate duplication of the flight path of the accident aircraft, the atmospheric conditions, the sun position, cloud cover, ground vegetation conditions, and with comparable power line conductor reflectance properties. All too frequently the geometry of the line, the terrain elevation properties with respect to tower locations, and the reflectance properties of the conductors, can lead to visibility conditions that cause aircraft wire strikes; the use of ball markers will greatly reduce the likelihood of the occurrence of such an accident.

Endnotes

1. "A Compendium of Aircraft Cockpit Vision Surveys 1950 Through 1980 Volume I," Anthony J. Barile, Report No. FAA-CT-81-40, Final Report, May 1981.

2. "Aeronautical Information Manual," U.S. Department of Transportation, Federal Aviation Administration, February 11, 2010.

3. "Midair Collision Avoidance, Your Role in Collision Avoidance," http://www.faa.gov/about/office_org/headquarters_offices/ato/tracon/anchorage/pilots_info/mca.

4. "'Avoid', The Unanalyzed Partner of 'See'," J. L. Harris, Sr., Forum, The International Society of Air Safety Investigators, Volume 16, No. 2, 1983.

5. "Validation Study of Wire-Strike Assessment Methodology," Southern California Edison Co. and Flight Safety Institute, Sacramento, CA 1992.

Appendix A

Midair Collision Worksheet

The purpose of this appendix is to pass along some of the details related to the Excel worksheets used to calculate the range and bearing information associated with two aircraft on a collision course based upon the radar data. Some readers may have no interest in this information, which is why it is included as an appendix. This would include readers who are not involved in generating this type of information, and those that make these types of calculations using a technique of their own development.

The Excel workbook consists of five worksheets. The first is for generating "Radar Error Boxes" documenting the radar accuracy limitations for the range, azimuth, and altitude information for each of the two aircraft. The second and third worksheets, one for each aircraft, involve the use of the radar data to make calculations related to the aircraft location, heading, bank, and pitch of each aircraft as a function of time until impact. The fourth and fifth worksheets utilize the previously generated data to calculate the bearing angles in azimuth and elevation from each aircraft to the other. Included herein are examples of each type of worksheet with explanations of the entries that are made to achieve the desired final product.

Worksheet 1, Radar Error Boxes

A copy of this worksheet, titled "Error Boxes," is shown below as Figure A.1. In this illustrative example, the printout covers the radar data for the last 22.5 seconds before impact to impact. The entire worksheet covers 60 seconds until impact. The two aircraft are designated as "AC1," columns B through G, and "AC2," columns H through M. The first two rows of the worksheet deal with the magnetic variation: the deviation of magnetic north from true north. In cell B1 the user enters this value in degrees and specifies the variation as either "East or West." The radar data reports the azimuth in terms of Azimuth Change Pulse counts (ACP's) where 4,096 ACP's = 360 degrees. In cell B2, the worksheet converts the Magnetic Variation in degrees to an ACP value by multiplying the

	A	B	C	D	E	F	G	H	I	J	K	L	M
1	Variation	13.37	deg	West									
2		152.12	ACPS	West									
3	21:03:50	Impact											
4	Time		Magnetic	TRUE	AC 1 X	AC 1 Y	AC 1 Z		Magnetic	TRUE	AC 2 X	AC 2 Y	AC 2 Z
5	Seconds	Range	ACP	ACP	Radar	Radar	Radar	Range	ACPs	ACP	Radar	Radar	Radar
6	0.0	24.250	449	296.88	10.687	21.907	1300	24.250	449	296.88	10.687	21.907	1300
7	0.0	24.250	449	296.88	10.754	21.874	1400	24.250	449	296.88	10.754	21.874	1400
8	0.0	24.250	449	296.88	10.644	21.650		24.250	449	296.88	10.644	21.650	
9	0.0	24.250	449	296.88	10.578	21.682		24.250	449	296.88	10.578	21.682	
10	0.0	24.250	449	296.88	10.687	21.907		24.250	449	296.88	10.687	21.907	
11													
12	4.5	24.250	445	292.88	10.553	21.972	1300	24.375	450	297.88	10.776	22.003	1300
13	4.5	24.250	445	292.88	10.620	21.940	1400	24.375	450	297.88	10.843	21.970	1400
14	4.5	24.250	445	292.88	10.511	21.715		24.375	450	297.88	10.733	21.746	
15	4.5	24.250	445	292.88	10.444	21.747		24.375	450	297.88	10.666	21.778	
16	4.5	24.250	445	292.88	10.553	21.972		24.375	450	297.88	10.776	22.003	
17													
18	9.0	24.250	440	287.88	10.384	22.053	1300	24.500	451	298.88	10.865	22.099	1300
19	9.0	24.250	440	287.88	10.451	22.021	1400	24.500	451	298.88	10.932	22.065	1400
20	9.0	24.250	440	287.88	10.344	21.795		24.500	451	298.88	10.821	21.841	
21	9.0	24.250	440	287.88	10.277	21.826		24.500	451	298.88	10.754	21.874	
22	9.0	24.250	440	287.88	10.384	22.053		24.500	451	298.88	10.865	22.099	
23													
24	13.5	24.250	436	283.88	10.248	22.116	1300	24.500	452	299.88	10.899	22.082	1400
25	13.5	24.250	436	283.88	10.316	22.084	1400	24.500	452	299.88	10.966	22.048	1500
26	13.5	24.250	436	283.88	10.210	21.858		24.500	452	299.88	10.855	21.825	
27	13.5	24.250	436	283.88	10.143	21.889		24.500	452	299.88	10.788	21.858	
28	13.5	24.250	436	283.88	10.248	22.116		24.500	452	299.88	10.899	22.082	
29													
30	18.0	24.250	432	279.88	10.112	22.178	1200	24.625	453	300.88	10.988	22.177	1400
31	18.0	24.250	432	279.88	10.180	22.147	1300	24.625	453	300.88	11.056	22.143	1500
32	18.0	24.250	432	279.88	10.076	21.920		24.625	453	300.88	10.944	21.920	
33	18.0	24.250	432	279.88	10.009	21.951		24.625	453	300.88	10.877	21.953	
34	18.0	24.250	432	279.88	10.112	22.178		24.625	453	300.88	10.988	22.177	
35													
36	22.5	24.125	428	275.88	9.925	22.126	1200	24.750	454	301.88	11.078	22.272	1400
37	22.5	24.125	428	275.88	9.993	22.095	1300	24.750	454	301.88	11.146	22.238	1500
38	22.5	24.125	428	275.88	9.890	21.868		24.750	454	301.88	11.034	22.015	
39	22.5	24.125	428	275.88	9.823	21.898		24.750	454	301.88	10.966	22.048	
40	22.5	24.125	428	275.88	9.925	22.126		24.750	454	301.88	11.078	22.272	

Figure A.1 *Spreadsheet used to generate the radar error boxes for the two aircraft in the illustrative example described in Chapter 4.*

numerical value in cell B1 by 4096/360. The user also enters the time of the impact: in this example "21:03:50" using the 24-hour clock, often referred to as "military time."

The user enters the radar data shown in Columns A, B, C and G (Time, Range, Azimuth ACP, and Altitude). In Columns A, B, C, and D, the radar data is repeated vertically in each column five times. The user also enters the reported altitude and, just below that, the altitude plus 100 (altitude accuracy) in Column G.

The following is a summary of the entries and formulas associated with the each of the columns, A through G, for rows 6 through 10. The repetition of data for the five vertical cells is done to facilitate graphing the results.

Column A, "Time Seconds"

Row 6 through 10—Entry is zero indicating last radar hit occurred at impact.

Column B, "Range"
Rows 6 through 10—Entry is the radar range in nautical miles for time zero.

Column C, "Magnetic ACP"
Rows 6 through 10—Entry is the radar azimuth in terms of Magnetic ACP.

Column D, "True ACP"
Worksheet computes True ACP from Magnetic ACP.
Cell Formulas
D6, "=C6-$B$2", D7, "=C7-$B$2", and so on through D10.

Column E, "AC1 X Radar"
Computes the X (east-west) radar error box values for the radar azimuth and elevation data
Cell Formulas
E6, =($B6+0.125)*sin(radians($D6-1)/4096*360)
  $B6+0.125 is radar range + $1/8$ nautical mile (range accuracy)
  $D6-1 is Radar Azimuth in ACP - 1 ACP (azimuth accuracy)
E7, =($B7+0.125)*sin(radians($D7+1)/4096*360)
  $B7+0.125 is radar range + $1/8$ nautical mile (range accuracy)
  $D7+1 is Radar Azimuth in ACP + 1 ACP (azimuth accuracy)
E8, =($B8-0.125)*sin(radians($D8+1)/4096*360)
  $B8-0.125 is radar range - $1/8$ nautical mile (range accuracy)
  $D8+1 is Radar Azimuth in ACP + 1 ACP (azimuth accuracy)
E9, =($B9-0.125)*sin(radians($D9-1)/4096*360)
  $B9-0.125 is radar range - $1/8$ nautical mile (range accuracy)
  $D9-1 is Radar Azimuth in ACP - 1 ACP (azimuth accuracy)
E10, =($B10+0.125)*sin(radians($D10-1)/4096*360)
  Repeat of E6 (first corner of the radar error box)

Column F, "AC1 Y Radar"
Computes the Y (north-south) radar error box values for the radar azimuth and elevation data
Cell Formulas
F6, =($B6+0.125)*cos(radians($D6-1)/4096*360)
  $B6+0.125 is radar range + $1/8$ nautical mile (range accuracy)
  $D6-1 is Radar Azimuth in ACP - 1 ACP (azimuth accuracy)
F7, =($B7+0.125)*cos(radians($D7+1)/4096*360)
  $B7+0.125 is radar range + $1/8$ nautical mile (range accuracy)
  $D7+1 is Radar Azimuth in ACP + 1 ACP (azimuth accuracy)

F8, =($B8-0.125)*cos(radians($D8+1)/4096*360)
  $B8-0.125 is radar range - $^{1}/_{8}$ nautical mile (range accuracy)
  $D8+1 is Radar Azimuth in ACP + 1 ACP (azimuth accuracy)
F9, =($B9-0.125)*cos(radians($D9-1)/4096*360)
  $B9-0.125 is radar range - $^{1}/_{8}$ nautical mile (range accuracy)
  $D9-1 is Radar Azimuth in ACP - 1 ACP (azimuth accuracy)
F10, =($B10+0.125)*cos(radians($D10-1)/4096*360)
  Repeat of E6 (first corner of the radar error box)

Column G, "AC1 Z Radar"
Cell Formulas
G6, User enters the radar altitude data (increments of 100)
  Lower bound of the altitude
G7, "=G6+100"
  Upper bound of the altitude

Columns H through M
Identical to Columns B through G for Aircraft 2

Worksheet 2, Aircraft 1
The next step is to use the radar error boxes to generate a reasonable approxima-
tion to the flight path for each aircraft. This is done with two worksheets titled
"AC1" and "AC2." A printout of the last 20 seconds of flight of the worksheet,
"AC1," is shown as Figure A.2.

Upper Worksheet Entries User Entries

Cell C3, Wind Velocity, knots
Cell D3, Wind Direction, True Azimuth

NOTE: The author is not an aeronautical engineer, though the author has com-
pleted a few courses dealing with these topics. Readers who are aeronautical
engineers may well have a better approach to calculating aircraft angle of attack
and pitch. The author's involvement in midair collisions is directed toward the
visibility issues. Fortunately, in all of the midair collisions investigated, the author has not had any instances where small changes in the pitch attitude of the
aircraft involved would have significantly altered the conclusions with respect to
the visibility issues related to the accident.

	A	B	C	D	E	F	G	H	I	J	K	L	M	N	O	P	Q
1	Aircraft 1		Wind														
2			Vel K Direction						Stall Speed =		49.5	kts					
3			17	270					Cruise Speed		113.0	kts					
4									Aspect Ratio = 6.2								
5			Wind Correction (ft per second)						AOA = AOA(Stall)/(Speed/Stall Speed)^2/cos(Bank)								
6			X	Y					Pitch = AOA - AOA(Cruise) + atan(Climb*60/(V(k)*6076/3600))								
7			29	0					AOA	18.00	deg	Pitch =	14.54	deg			
8			Wind Correction (nm/sec)						AOA	3.46	deg	Pitch =	0.00	deg			
9			X	Y													
10			0	0													
11	Impact at 21:03:50												TRUE				
12	Clock	T	dT	V(k)	dV(k)	C	dC	B	dB	X Calc	Y Calc	Z Calc	H	dH	R	AOA	Pitch
13	21:03:50	0.0		112.00		100		0		10.679	21.805	1327	111.00		0.0	3.52	0.57
14	21:03:50	0.5	0.5	112.00	0.00	100	0	0	0	10.66	21.81	1326	111.00	0.0	0.0	3.52	0.57
15	21:03:49	1.0	0.5	112.00	0.00	100	0	0	0	10.65	21.82	1325	111.00	0.0	0.0	3.52	0.57
16	21:03:49	1.5	0.5	112.00	0.00	100	0	0	0	10.63	21.82	1325	111.00	0.0	0.0	3.52	0.57
17	21:03:48	2.0	0.5	112.00	0.00	100	0	0	0	10.61	21.83	1324	111.00	0.0	0.0	3.52	0.57
18	21:03:48	2.5	0.5	112.00	0.00	100	0	0	0	10.59	21.83	1323	111.00	0.0	0.0	3.52	0.57
19	21:03:47	3.0	0.5	112.00	0.00	100	0	0	0	10.58	21.84	1322	111.00	0.0	0.0	3.52	0.57
20	21:03:47	3.5	0.5	112.00	0.00	100	0	0	0	10.56	21.84	1321	111.00	0.0	0.0	3.52	0.57
21	21:03:46	4.0	0.5	112.00	0.00	100	0	0	0	10.54	21.85	1320	111.00	0.0	0.0	3.52	0.57
22	21:03:46	4.5	0.5	112.00	0.00	100	0	0	0	10.53	21.86	1320	111.00	0.0	0.0	3.52	0.57
23	21:03:45	5.0	0.5	112.00	0.00	100	0	0	0	10.51	21.86	1319	111.00	0.0	0.0	3.52	0.57
24	21:03:45	5.5	0.5	112.00	0.00	100	0	0	0	10.49	21.87	1318	111.00	0.0	0.0	3.52	0.57
25	21:03:44	6.0	0.5	112.00	0.00	100	0	0	0	10.48	21.87	1317	111.00	0.0	0.0	3.52	0.57
26	21:03:44	6.5	0.5	112.00	0.00	100	0	0	0	10.46	21.88	1316	111.00	0.0	0.0	3.52	0.57
27	21:03:43	7.0	0.5	112.00	0.00	100	0	0	0	10.44	21.88	1315	111.00	0.0	0.0	3.52	0.57
28	21:03:43	7.5	0.5	112.00	0.00	100	0	0	0	10.43	21.89	1315	111.00	0.0	0.0	3.52	0.57
29	21:03:42	8.0	0.5	112.00	0.00	100	0	0	0	10.41	21.89	1314	111.00	0.0	0.0	3.52	0.57
30	21:03:42	8.5	0.5	112.00	0.00	100	0	0	0	10.39	21.90	1313	111.00	0.0	0.0	3.52	0.57
31	21:03:41	9.0	0.5	112.00	0.00	100	0	0	0	10.38	21.91	1312	111.00	0.0	0.0	3.52	0.57
32	21:03:41	9.5	0.5	112.00	0.00	100	0	0	0	10.36	21.91	1311	111.00	0.0	0.0	3.52	0.57
33	21:03:40	10.0	0.5	112.00	0.00	100	0	0	0	10.34	21.92	1310	111.00	0.0	0.0	3.52	0.57
34	21:03:40	10.5	0.5	112.00	0.00	100	0	0	0	10.32	21.92	1310	111.00	0.0	0.0	3.52	0.57
35	21:03:39	11.0	0.5	112.00	0.00	100	0	0	0	10.31	21.93	1309	111.00	0.0	0.0	3.52	0.57
36	21:03:39	11.5	0.5	112.00	0.00	100	0	0	0	10.29	21.93	1308	111.00	0.0	0.0	3.52	0.57
37	21:03:38	12.0	0.5	112.00	0.00	100	0	0	0	10.27	21.94	1307	111.00	0.0	0.0	3.52	0.57
38	21:03:38	12.5	0.5	112.00	0.00	100	0	0	0	10.26	21.94	1306	111.00	0.0	0.0	3.52	0.57
39	21:03:37	13.0	0.5	112.00	0.00	100	0	0	0	10.24	21.95	1305	111.00	0.0	0.0	3.52	0.57
40	21:03:37	13.5	0.5	112.00	0.00	100	0	0	0	10.22	21.96	1305	111.00	0.0	0.0	3.52	0.57
41	21:03:36	14.0	0.5	112.00	0.00	100	0	0	0	10.21	21.96	1304	111.00	0.0	0.0	3.52	0.57
42	21:03:36	14.5	0.5	112.00	0.00	100	0	0	0	10.19	21.97	1303	111.00	0.0	0.0	3.52	0.57
43	21:03:35	15.0	0.5	112.00	0.00	100	0	0	0	10.17	21.97	1302	111.00	0.0	0.0	3.52	0.57
44	21:03:35	15.5	0.5	112.00	0.00	100	0	0	0	10.16	21.98	1301	111.00	0.0	0.0	3.52	0.57
45	21:03:34	16.0	0.5	112.00	0.00	100	0	0	0	10.14	21.98	1300	111.00	0.0	0.0	3.52	0.57
46	21:03:34	16.5	0.5	112.00	0.00	100	0	0	0	10.12	21.99	1300	111.00	0.0	0.0	3.52	0.57
47	21:03:33	17.0	0.5	112.00	0.00	100	0	0	0	10.10	21.99	1299	111.00	0.0	0.0	3.52	0.57
48	21:03:33	17.5	0.5	112.00	0.00	100	0	0	0	10.09	22.00	1298	111.00	0.0	0.0	3.52	0.57
49	21:03:32	18.0	0.5	112.00	0.00	100	0	15	15	10.07	22.01	1297	110.35	-0.7	2.6	3.64	0.69
50	21:03:32	18.5	0.5	112.00	0.00	100	0	30	15	10.05	22.01	1296	108.28	-2.1	5.6	4.07	1.11
51	21:03:31	19.0	0.5	112.00	0.00	100	0	30	0	10.04	22.02	1295	105.47	-2.8	5.6	4.07	1.11
52	21:03:31	19.5	0.5	112.00	0.00	100	0	30	0	10.02	22.02	1295	102.65	-2.8	5.6	4.07	1.11
53	21:03:30	20.0	0.5	112.00	0.00	100	0	30	0	10.00	22.02	1294	99.83	-2.8	5.6	4.07	1.11

Figure A.2 Spreadsheet used to generate the flight path for aircraft 1 in the illustrative example described in Chapter 4.

Cell K2, Enter Stall Speed, knots

Cell K3, Enter Cruise Speed, knots

Cell K4, Enter Aspect Ratio (Wing Length to Breadth)

Cell J7, Enter angle of attack, stall speed

Cell M8, Enter Pitch at Cruise Speed

Cell Formulas:

Cell C7, "=C3*6076/3600*sin(radians(D3-180))"

Calculates the wind velocity in feet per second in the "X" direction

Cell D7, "=C3*6076/3600*cos(radians(D3-180))"

Calculates the wind velocity in feet per second in the "Y " direction

Cell C10, "=C7/6076"

Converts "X" wind velocity to nautical miles per second

Cell D10, "=D7/6076"

Converts "Y" wind velocity to nautical miles per second

Cell J8, "=J7/((K3/K2)^2"

Calculates Angle of Attack at cruise speed

Cell M7, "J7-J8"

Calculates Pitch at Stall

Main Worksheet AC1 Cell Entries and Formulas for Entries Made on Row 13 to Initiate the Calculations

A13 Impact military clock time

B13 Enter 0 for T (time to impact)

D13 Enter velocity at impact in knots

F13 Enter climb rate at impact in feet per minute

H13 Enter Bank angle at impact in degrees (positive to the right)

J13 Enter X (east-west) distance in nm from the radar site at impact

K13 Enter Y(north-south) distance in nm from the radar site at impact

L13 Enter altitude at impact

M13 Enter aircraft heading at impact

Cell Formulas for row 13

Cell O13, "=360/(2*pi)*32.2*tan(radians(H13))/(D13*6076/3600))"

Calculates heading change (deg/sec) for bank angle and velocity

Cell P13, "=If(D13>$K$2,$J*7/(D13/$K$2)^2/cos(radians(H13)),$J$7)"

Calculates angle of attack based on airspeed and bank angle

Cell Q13, "=P13-$J$8+degrees(atan(F13/60)/(D13*6076/3600)))"

Calculates pitch based on angle of attack, velocity and bank angle

Cell Formulas and entries for row 14

Cell A14, "=A13-(B14-B13)/(3600*24)"

Calculates clock time based on time difference from previous row

Cell B14, "=B13+0.5"

Calculates time until impact based on chosen time interval (0.5 sec)

Cell C14, "=B14-B13"

Calculates the difference in time for last two entries

Cell D14, "=D13+E14"

Calculates the new velocity in knots

Cell E14, Enter change in velocity in knots

Cell F14, "=F13+G14"

Calculates the new climb rate feet per minute

Cell G14, Enter the change in climb rate feet per minute

Cell H14, "=H13+I14"

Calculates the new bank angle in degrees (positive to right)

Cell I14, Enter the change in bank angle in degrees (positive to right)

Cell J14,"=J13-($D13+$D14)/2/3600*$C14*sin(radians(($M13+$M14)/2))
*sin(radians($N14)+0.000001)/($N14*pi()/180+0.000001)-
$C$10*$C14

Calculates the X (east-west) distance, nautical miles

Cell K14,"=K13-($D13+$D14)/2/3600*$C14*cos(radians(($M13+$M14)/
2))*sin(radians($N14)+0.000001)/($N14*pi()/180+0.000001)-
$C$10*$C14

Calculates the Y (north-south) distance, nautical miles

Cell L14, "=L13-(F13+F14)/2/60*C14"

Calculates the Z (altitude) in feet

Cell M14, "=M13-(O13+O14)/2*C14"

Calculates the heading in degrees

Cell N14, "=M14-M13"

Calculates the change in heading in degrees

Cell O14, "=Degrees(32.2*tan(radians(H14)/(D14*6076/3600))

Calculates the heading change in degrees per second

Cell P14, "=If(D14>$K$2,$J$7/(D14/$K$2)^2/cos(radians(H14)),$J$7)"

Calculates the angle of attack in degrees

Cll Q14, "=P14-$J$8+degrees(atan(F14/60/(D14*6076/3600)))"

Calculates the pitch angle in degrees

To generate all rows greater than row 14, copy row 14 and paste to as many additional rows as desired. The entire worksheet can be copied and pasted to a second worksheet (AC2) to be used for Aircraft 2.

The third worksheet is titled AC1-AC2 FOV. It uses the two worksheets, AC1 and AC2 to calculate the bearing angles of the path of sight from Aircraft 1 to Aircraft 2. A copy of the last 20 seconds before impact for this worksheet is shown as Figure A.3.

Entries made on row 4 to initiate the calculations

A4 Impact military clock time

B4 Enter 0 for T (time to impact)

Cell Formulas for row 5

Cell A5, "='AC1'!A14"

Copies the time from Worksheet AC1

Cell B5, "=B4+0.5"

Calculates the chosen time until impact in seconds

Cell C5, "='AC2'!J14-'AC1'!J14"

Calculates the difference in X positions for the two aircraft

Cell D5, "='AC2'!K14-'AC1'!K14"

Calculates the difference in Y positions for the two aircraft

Cell E5, "='AC2'!L14-'AC1'!L14"

Calculates the difference in altitude of the two aircraft

Cell F5, "=sqrt(C5^2+D5^2)"

Calculates the range between the two aircraft in nautical miles

Cell G5, "=Degrees(atan2(D5,C5))"

Calculates the true azimuth of line of sight from AC1 to AC2

Cell H5, "=G5-'AC1'!M14"

Calculates the bearing angle between AC1 and AC2

Cell I5, "=F5*sin(radians(H5))"

Calculates the distance of AC2 left or right of the heading of AC1

Cell J5, "=F5*cos(radians(H5))"

Calculates the distance of AC2 perpendicular to heading of AC1

Cell K5, "=E5"

Duplication of Cell E5, difference in altitude of two aircraft

Cell L5, "=degrees(atan(K5/(F5*6076)))"

Calculates elevation angle of path of sight from AC1 to AC2

Cell M5, "=sqrt(H5^2+L5^2)*sin(atan(H5/L5)-radians('AC1'!H14))"

Calculates the azimuth bearing angle for bank angle of AC1

Cell N5, "=sqrt(H5^2+L5^2)*cos(atan(H5/L5)-radians('AC1'!H14))-'AC1'!Q13"

Calculation elevation bearing angle for banks angle of AC1

	A	B	C	D	E	F	G	H	I	J	K	L	M	N
1	AC1 Bearing Angles to AC2													
2														
3	Time	T	dX	dY	dZ	R(x,y)	AZ0	AZ1	dX	dY	dZ	EL1	AZ2	EL2
4	21:03:50	0.0												
5	21:03:50	0.5	0.025	0.001	4	0.025	86.9	-24.096	-0.010	0.022	4.2	1.599	-24.10	1.03
6	21:03:49	1.0	0.049	0.003	8	0.049	86.9	-24.096	-0.020	0.045	8.3	1.599	-24.10	1.03
7	21:03:49	1.5	0.074	0.004	12	0.074	86.9	-24.096	-0.030	0.067	12.5	1.599	-24.10	1.03
8	21:03:48	2.0	0.098	0.005	17	0.098	86.9	-24.096	-0.040	0.090	16.7	1.599	-24.10	1.03
9	21:03:48	2.5	0.123	0.007	21	0.123	86.9	-24.096	-0.050	0.112	20.8	1.599	-24.10	1.03
10	21:03:47	3.0	0.147	0.008	25	0.147	86.9	-24.096	-0.060	0.135	25.0	1.599	-24.10	1.03
11	21:03:47	3.5	0.172	0.009	29	0.172	86.9	-24.096	-0.070	0.157	29.2	1.599	-24.10	1.03
12	21:03:46	4.0	0.196	0.011	33	0.196	86.9	-24.096	-0.080	0.179	33.3	1.599	-24.10	1.03
13	21:03:46	4.5	0.221	0.012	37	0.221	86.9	-24.096	-0.090	0.202	37.5	1.599	-24.10	1.03
14	21:03:45	5.0	0.245	0.013	42	0.246	86.9	-24.096	-0.100	0.224	41.7	1.599	-24.10	1.03
15	21:03:45	5.5	0.270	0.015	46	0.270	86.9	-24.096	-0.110	0.247	45.8	1.599	-24.10	1.03
16	21:03:44	6.0	0.294	0.016	50	0.295	86.9	-24.096	-0.120	0.269	50.0	1.599	-24.10	1.03
17	21:03:44	6.5	0.319	0.017	54	0.319	86.9	-24.096	-0.130	0.291	54.2	1.599	-24.10	1.03
18	21:03:43	7.0	0.343	0.018	58	0.344	86.9	-24.096	-0.140	0.314	58.3	1.599	-24.10	1.03
19	21:03:43	7.5	0.368	0.020	62	0.368	86.9	-24.096	-0.150	0.336	62.5	1.599	-24.10	1.03
20	21:03:42	8.0	0.392	0.021	67	0.393	86.9	-24.096	-0.160	0.359	66.7	1.599	-24.10	1.03
21	21:03:42	8.5	0.417	0.023	71	0.418	86.9	-24.096	-0.170	0.381	70.8	1.599	-24.10	1.03
22	21:03:41	9.0	0.441	0.024	75	0.442	86.9	-24.096	-0.180	0.404	75.0	1.599	-24.10	1.03
23	21:03:41	9.5	0.466	0.025	79	0.467	86.9	-24.096	-0.191	0.426	79.2	1.599	-24.10	1.03
24	21:03:40	10.0	0.490	0.027	83	0.491	86.9	-24.096	-0.201	0.448	83.3	1.599	-24.10	1.03
25	21:03:40	10.5	0.515	0.028	87	0.516	86.9	-24.096	-0.211	0.471	87.5	1.599	-24.10	1.03
26	21:03:39	11.0	0.540	0.029	92	0.540	86.9	-24.096	-0.221	0.493	91.7	1.599	-24.10	1.03
27	21:03:39	11.5	0.564	0.031	96	0.565	86.9	-24.096	-0.231	0.516	95.8	1.599	-24.10	1.03
28	21:03:38	12.0	0.589	0.032	100	0.589	86.9	-24.096	-0.241	0.538	100.0	1.599	-24.10	1.03
29	21:03:38	12.5	0.613	0.033	104	0.614	86.9	-24.096	-0.251	0.561	104.2	1.599	-24.10	1.03
30	21:03:37	13.0	0.638	0.034	108	0.639	86.9	-24.096	-0.261	0.583	108.3	1.599	-24.10	1.03
31	21:03:37	13.5	0.662	0.036	111	0.663	86.9	-24.096	-0.271	0.605	110.8	1.576	-24.10	1.01
32	21:03:36	14.0	0.687	0.037	112	0.688	86.9	-24.096	-0.281	0.628	111.7	1.531	-24.10	0.97
33	21:03:36	14.5	0.711	0.038	112	0.712	86.9	-24.096	-0.291	0.650	112.5	1.489	-24.10	0.92
34	21:03:35	15.0	0.736	0.040	113	0.737	86.9	-24.096	-0.301	0.673	113.3	1.450	-24.10	0.88
35	21:03:35	15.5	0.760	0.041	114	0.761	86.9	-24.096	-0.311	0.695	114.2	1.414	-24.10	0.85
36	21:03:34	16.0	0.785	0.042	115	0.786	86.9	-24.096	-0.321	0.717	115.0	1.380	-24.10	0.81
37	21:03:34	16.5	0.809	0.044	116	0.810	86.9	-24.096	-0.331	0.740	115.8	1.347	-24.10	0.78
38	21:03:33	17.0	0.834	0.045	117	0.835	86.9	-24.096	-0.341	0.762	116.7	1.317	-24.10	0.75
39	21:03:33	17.5	0.858	0.047	117	0.860	86.9	-24.096	-0.351	0.785	117.5	1.289	-24.10	0.72
40	21:03:32	18.0	0.883	0.048	118	0.884	86.9	-23.447	-0.352	0.811	118.3	1.262	-22.97	-5.42
41	21:03:32	18.5	0.908	0.050	119	0.909	86.9	-21.411	-0.332	0.846	119.2	1.236	-19.16	-10.32
42	21:03:31	19.0	0.932	0.052	120	0.934	86.8	-18.656	-0.299	0.885	120.0	1.211	-16.76	-9.39
43	21:03:31	19.5	0.958	0.055	121	0.959	86.7	-15.942	-0.263	0.922	120.8	1.188	-14.40	-8.05
44	21:03:30	20.0	0.983	0.059	122	0.985	86.6	-13.265	-0.226	0.958	121.7	1.165	-12.07	-6.73

Figure A.3 Spreadsheet used to calculate the bearing angles from aircraft 1 to aircraft 2 in the illustrative example described in Chapter 4.

To generate all rows greater than row 5, copy row 5 and paste to all of the rows necessary to include all data rows of Worksheet AC1. The entire worksheet can be copied and pasted to a fifth worksheet to create a similar worksheet for AC2-AC1 FOV.

These five worksheets provide the calculations necessary to generate the illustrative graphs shown in Chapter 4.

About the Authors

James L. Harris, Sr. served in the military from 1944 to 1946, and again during the Korean War from 1950 to 1952. He received a Bronze Star for his service in Korea. He obtained a B.S. degree in Electrical Engineering from Iowa State College in 1949. Following his second military tour he was employed by the Willow Run Research Center, University of Michigan from 1952 to 1954. He worked on the design of radar systems for active missile defense during that period. In 1954 he joined the staff of the Visibility Laboratory, Scripps Institution of Oceanography, University of California where he served for 25 years. During that period he held various positions including Branch Head, Manager of Research, Associate Director, and Director. He held appointments as a lecturer with the Department of Applied Physics and Information Science Department, UCSD. His primary research activities at the Visibility Laboratory included research as to the capabilities and limitations of all types of light-sensing devices, the development of computer techniques for the extraction of reliable data from photographs, and the application of the labs vision research data to the topic of visibility and visual search in real-world situations. During his tenure at the Visibility Laboratory he received annual appointments for 20 years to membership in the National Academy of Science, National Research Council, Committee on Vision. He was an invited speaker at three national seminars sponsored by the Vision Committee where he presented lectures on visual search. He was elected to the Board of Directors of the Optical Society of America and served as their official lecturer for a two-year period. The Visibility Laboratory was named by NASA as the lead laboratory in studies made during two Gemini space flights to determine whether prolonged weightlessness resulted in a reduction in the visual acuity of the astronauts. Those contacts resulted in his being named Principal Investigator in a series of grants from NASA to study the role of vision in aircraft midair collisions. In 1971 that research led to his being called by the Department of Justice as an expert in litigation associated with an aircraft midair collision. Since that time, he has been retained as an expert in over 120 midair collisions. He became Director Emeritus of the Visibility Laboratory when he accepted an early retirement in 1979 and formed Harris Visibility Studies, Inc. He has served as an expert in over 1,000 cases involving the analysis of visibility issues in all types of accidents, each of which involved questions as to whether the parties involved would have been able to visually acquire information that would have allowed them to avoid the accident.

James L. Harris II began working part-time for Harris Visibility Studies, Inc. in 1979 while he was still in high school. During his tenure with HVSI from 1979 to 1985 he took course work that included Computer Animation, 3-D Modeling, Animation and Rendering, and Autodesk 3D Studio Modeling, Animation and Rendering. He entered the Air Force in 1985 and received training as a Jet Engine Mechanic. He finished his Air Force tour in 1988 and joined the staff of the North Island Naval Air Station Depot in Aircraft Engine Repair. In 1991 he rejoined his father at Harris Visibility Studies, Inc. He played a primary role in photography and video recording, light measurements, accident site visits, calculations of sun and moon conditions, courtroom exhibit preparations, computer image processing, and 3D Studios computer animation and simulation. In 1992 he co-authored, with his father, a paper titled "Forensic Photography and Nighttime Visibility Issues," *Journal of Forensic Sciences*, July 1992. In 2008 he and his father began to discuss the possibility of writing a book on forensic visibility. They held lengthy discussions, generated outlines, and did exploratory writing and planning as to the appropriate content of such a publication. He was an extremely important member of the HVSI team until his untimely death in August 2009.

Index

CPSIA information can be obtained at www.ICGtesting.com
Printed in the USA
BVOW041630181211

278641BV00002B/7/P